THE
NCG
FACTOR™

A Formula for Building Life-Changing
Relationships from College to Retirement

LARRY KAUFMAN

THE **NCG** FACTOR

Cover Design by Juan Pablo Ruiz
Printed in the United States of America

ISBN: 978-1-7330635-1-7

FIG
FACTOR
MEDIA

CONTENTS

TESTIMONIALS

"I have had the honor to witness the amazing impact of NCG personally with my interactions with Larry Kaufman. The NCG formula has provided me with unique opportunities to build life-changing relationships and friendships, inspiring me to become a more caring and giving individual. It has had a profound impact on my life!"

GLENN A. NADELL, Family Office CEO & Lawyer, Glenn A. Nadell Consulting Services

"When you are connected to a person as gifted as Larry, who is a natural giver, you really never have to ask for help. He's just always there, unselfishly putting his network to use to help you at critical points in time. Watching Larry use the NCG principles has inspired me to get more involved with my own network and help others succeed."

JIM DIMITRIOU, Sales Market Leader Central Region, Advisory Services, BDO

"I've experienced the power of the NCG Factor and found that connecting with others more deeply and giving and is not only a great strategy for living a more successful, fulfilling life... It's what the world needs a whole lot more of right now. I'm a BIG FAN!"

JON BUTCHER, Chairman of the Precious Moments Family of Companies and Founder of Lifebook

"NCG has been the blueprint for my entrepreneurial success. I have learned that my network equals my net worth. The principals of NCG have made a huge impact on me, and in turn, thousands of people in my companies that I have been able to help. Thank you, Larry!"

JEFF ELLMAN, Co-Founder, Hireology and UrbanBound

"NCG Factor shows you how to "Pay-it-Forward" in today's fast-paced business world. Larry's approach to investing small, consistent quality time helping people in transition is a skill that should be learned and applied for anyone wanting to enrich their lives with life-changing relationships and friendships. NCG Factor shows you a new creative roadmap to a meaningful legacy of GIVING. This timeless skill has made all the difference in my own life, which has been rewarding beyond measure."

MARK SLABY, Investor and Entrepreneur, Founder of Juno Payments, Co-founder of Patriot Education Fund

I am dedicating this book to my wife, Charmaine, who has been with me for 30 years and encouraged me to invest in myself and write this book, as well as my son, Matthew, and daughter, Nicole. They have given me the inspiration to be the best I can be for my family and for others, every day.

ACKNOWLEDGEMENTS

I would like to express my gratitude to the following people who are my "life-changing relationships"....

My wife, **Charmaine**, who married me in Las Vegas in 1989 and loved and supported me throughout the finishing of this book. Yes, she is mentioned twice!

All my NCG Masters who lent their words to this book. They are profiled in the "Meet the NCG Masters" page and include: **Peter K. Braxton, Desmond Clark, Zori Haouchine, Don Hyun Kiolbassa, Steve Kosmalski, Robert Kunz, Lesly Marban, Michael Quig, Ed Toczyski, Michael Verden, Gregg Salkovitch and Megan Wessels.**

Jon Butcher, Jim Dimitriou, Jeff Ellman, Glenn A. Nadell, and Mark Slaby who kindly endorsed this book.

Bryan Sugar, the first connector in my life, who made me take action to become a connector.

Mary Erlain, who changed my life when she asked me to present about LinkedIn for the first time to a group of small business owners.

Karen Andrews, an early connector who introduced me to Mary Erlain.

Brenda Dunn Kinney, one of the very first connectors in my life who continues to be a connector in my life.

Michael Hahn, a great connector for me and to Fig Factor Media and their team.

Jackie Camacho-Ruiz, the pilot for this book, which was a smooth flight with no turbulence.

Karen Dix of Fig Factor Media, my NCG Muse

Chad Coe, who wrote my forward and is a giver, connector and so much more.

Desmond Clark, who made an introduction for my son to the Blackhawks for a very special and memorable meet and greet with Jonathan Toews and Patrick Kane. Truly life-changing for my son!

Mike Lauesen, who helped me to become a Vistage-approved speaker and so much more.

Morrie Elstien, the connector of connectors I wish I had met when I was in college.

Gregg Elstien, another great connector and chip off the old block.

Cindi Elstien, who completes the family of great connectors.

Bob Arthur, who went out of his way to leverage his relationships to help my son.

George Kelly, who brought me back to an incredible leadership role working for a great boss.

Brandt Kucharski, who challenged me to support Holiday Heroes and later joined the Board, which has been truly life changing.

Stuart Baum, a giver, who made public accounting feel like a real partnership.

Mike Flynn, a LinkedIn champion of mine.

Bonnie Kaplan, an ultra-giver and connector.

Jonathan Rothstein, a fellow connector.

Tricia Meyer, one of the greatest attorney connectors I know.
Gene Rosendale, a great "neuro" connector.
John Kringas, the world's best photographer.
Tom Goldblatt, who never says no.
Tom Moran, a giver at a critical time in my career.

I would also like to thank so many that have helped me along the way with connections, giving hearts and their friendship. These include **Judson Kinnucan, Sandra Noworul, Frank Cesario, Steve Brown, Allen Caviles, David Hirsh, Patrick Beharelle, Allen Carter, Dave Franckowiak, Brian LeVay, John Ambrogi, Dan Garms, Dan Martin, Dan Cotter, Bill Finn, Marty Koehler, Rob Tovar, Gayle Norton, Janeen McGreal, Adrian Dinu, Allison Sima, Dan Gallas, Steve Schaumberger, Matt O'Sullivan, John Scully, Allen Carter, Leslie Anderson, Joe Kelsch, Brent Novoselsky, Bill Zanoni, Gregory Gordon, Steve Thomas, Jon Reinsdorf, Ron Repking, Josh Spencer, Jeff Rosset, Mark Miller, Peter Rudman, John Ruh, Jeff Steigelman, Paul Carlisle, Kathleen McCann-Battle, Michael Stuart, Peter Davidson, Quinton James, Christine Johnson, Steve Adelstein, Dan Yunker, Ed Dernulc, Steve Callisher, George Smith, Rick Hernandez, Brian Bries, Matt Croll, Brian Meade, Judy Foley, Jeff Froman, Dr. Mark Frigo, Eileen Timmins, Lou Costabile, George Boyadjis, John Barton, Sharon Noha, Clyde Lowstuter, Paul Duski, Adam Gelfeld, Andrew Boron, Julie West, Jim Vaselopulos, Joel Goldblatt** and so many more who have changed my life.

FOREWORD
By Chad Coe

Why, you might wonder, would I—a financial advisor, author, and charity auctioneer—write a preface for this book?

Because when Larry and I met each other twenty years ago at a networking meeting, it was like a cosmic collision. We were two NCG masters meeting each other and we recognized it right away because we shared a special energy. We kept interrupting each other in conversation, saying things like, "What do you need?" soon followed by, "I have someone you should meet," and "I just met with someone who needs someone like you..."

This kind of relationship continued for years, which is no surprise. When you meet someone who truly understands the power of networking, connecting, and giving, they are usually in your life forever. You also often find yourself drawn together at some very crucial life moments.

When Larry was in transition, I met with him to share some important contacts to help him find his next opportunity. During our collaborative 1:1 meetings, we would share opportunities that came our way and discuss how we could help each other. When my son lost his first job, Larry was there to help and support us. He made some introductions that helped my son secure his current position working in finance and led him to become financially secure and reach his career goals.

As the author of three books *(The Power of Peopletizing, The Confident Leader, and the Auctioneer's Apprentice)* and founder of the Special Kid's Network, I've learned that in connecting and giving, we receive. This is true, even if you did it years ago and don't even remember! And that happens more often than we can imagine.

For example, I was approached by a lady recently who recognized me from another event. "I know you!" she said, her eyes lighting up. "You're a charity auctioneer, right?" I often get recognized for my auctioneering, so that wasn't surprising. But the event had taken place almost ten years ago! Even more surprising was what she told me next. Apparently, something I said on that night had inspired her to start her own charity! Like I've said in my own books, and as Larry and NCG can attest, you never know how far your connecting can go. And the fact that I was remembered all those years for sparking the idea lets me know that the world needs more connectors!

Larry's book is a great guide to learn to be that connector (as well as networker and giver) for those around us. I personally take the "G"—the giver part of "NCG" very personally. People will describe me as a gift giver. It's one of the secrets of being a confident leader. I carry small gift cards to reward those that go over and above, and whenever I can, I consider thoughtful gifts for those in my life. Being a giver inspires other people to give as well.

The "Special Kid's Network" has always been my baby,

with my wife in the co-pilot seat. At first, she didn't always understand the importance of it all, but was at my side at every gala event. One year, she had the chance to meet, and be thoroughly charmed, by some of the children involved in the charity. As we were preparing for the upcoming gala, she decided to select and order a pile of gifts through Amazon to present to the children attending that year. When the evening of the big event arrived, she walked into the sparkling ballroom and one of the first things she beheld was a beautiful little girl. The girl's smile was shining as brightly as the chandeliers and she was filled with joy, hugging a stack of gifts that my wife had purchased. When my wife realized what was happening, she was overcome with happiness. A connection had led to a giving opportunity that had changed two lives forever!

It works the same way in the business world. Through the years, I've given to others in a lot of different ways. I've helped people find jobs and make important connections. And I've watched people cry when they've had a life-altering epiphany about their life's purpose, because as Mark Twain said, "The two most important days in your life are the day you are born and the day you find out why."

Giving takes strength, but that strength can be nurtured by networking and connecting. Work to give to others every day, through your connections, your personal calling, or your financial good fortune. The result will be more powerful than you can ever imagine.

Larry knows all this, which is why *The NCG Factor* is here to help us all. Even better, it can help you from college to retirement. Larry has found his path in his journey and has created a legacy as an unselfish giver to others. This book is yet another testament to Larry's giving, and it's a gift we all must share with each other.

Happy Reading!

-Chad Coe

President & CEO, Coe Financial Group, Keynote Speaker on Leadership & Sales, Benefit Auctioneer, Author, *The Auctioneer's Apprentice, The Confident Leader, The Power of Peopletizing*

INTRODUCTION

When you have a secret, sometimes it's better to share it! The NCG Factor is one such secret, a powerful formula for successful relationship building that has truly changed my life. That's why I'm writing this book; so you too, can change your life with the NCG Factor!

When I was in college, and later venturing out as a young grad, I could have used this book, but there wasn't anything like it available. Yet the beauty of the NCG Factor is that it is useful for anyone, at any time of life, which is why this book addresses the life-long relevance of the NCG Factor from college to retirement. No matter how young or old we are, whether we are a professional newbie or a seasoned industry veteran, reading this book can save you from making the relationship-building mistakes I have made over the years. The NCG Factor can help you start building a legacy as a giver to others...today!

I have to admit that I could not have achieved what I have, personally and professionally, without the NCG Factor! Throughout my life, I've developed countless new clients and created revenue for my companies thanks to the introductions I received to CEO's, CFO's, CHRO's, etc., courtesy of the NCG Factor. It's helped me meet amazing people that I, in turn, was able to introduce to others.

And it has also helped me throughout my life. I have easily secured speaking engagements on LinkedIn just by leveraging the principles of NCG. When I found myself in transition, I turned to NCG to help me find my next career position. I live and engage the limitless power of The NCG Factor every day of my life, personally and professionally, and once you do too, the results will be life-changing. I promise!

This book has two parts: an introduction to the concept of NCG, which applies to everyone, and a special section on how to use the NCG Factor in each phase of your life from college to retirement. At the back of the book, there is also an "NCG Action List" to jumpstart your NCG efforts. My hope is that this book becomes your guide through life (whatever phase you are in) and a resource to pass on to friends and family too.

The NCG Factor has been nothing less than transformative in my life and has helped me rewrite my legacy! If it does the same for you, please let me know. Get in touch and share your story. Together, we can spread the word about the NCG Factor!

All my best,

Larry Kaufman
kaufman_34@hotmail.com
(847) 226-5398

PROLOGUE
Meet the NCG Masters

Throughout this book, I will be referring to and quoting my "NCG Masters." These are recent or life-long relationships in my network who have so graciously contributed their wisdom and experiences to this book to show how to successfully apply the NCG Factor in real life. All of them started out as business connections, but over the years, have become friends who are an important part of my inner circle. In a way, they make up a cast of characters for this book. I'm grateful to each and every one of them. Without their support and belief in my mission, this book would not be possible.

Peter K. Braxton is a Director/Business Development Executive for ENVOI, a multi-family office financial services firm, and a military veteran and former U.S. Air Force combat pilot. He also has the distinction of being the first military jet and first refueling jet to arrive in New York during 911. Peter is also an NCG Master. Peter and I instantly clicked when we met through a mutual friend.

Desmond Clark is a former tight end (number 88) for the Chicago Bears who transitioned into a career as a financial advisor when he retired from football at age thirty-four. We met at the beginning of his transition. I helped him develop into a masterful user of NCG and helped him make connections in his professional life. See Chapter 5 for how Desmond made a big difference in my life!

Zori Haouchine is the Founder and Creative Director of her own firm, ZOHA Architecture + Design, and has made the NCG Factor work for her in a very meaningful way. Zori and I met through a friend to help her expand her network for her new business. She is from another country with different values and doesn't take the opportunities offered in the United States for granted.

Don Hyun Kiolbassa is a CPA and attorney who also happens to be a martial arts gold medalist and an action model for Mortal Kombat! Don leverages NCG well and has been receptive to my introductions, while I have been receptive to his requests too.

Steve Kosmalski is the former CEO and board member of Precious Moments, Inc.

Steve has served as a CEO for other companies throughout his career and we met at a networking event when he was looking for his next CEO role. He was good with NCG then and still is today. His experience and positive attitude make him a person you want to help.

Robert Kunz is a successful producer at Gallagher but I knew him when he was a summer intern after his junior year at Miami University. He quickly learned how to apply the NCG formula and contributes his past experience as a college intern to this book.

Lesly Marban is the Principal at Diberin Solutions, LLC, a management consulting company. Leslie was formerly a CMO for a $10 billion corporation in the medical industry. She is a long-time master of NCG and her friendly demeanor and willingness to help others make it easy to help Lesly.

Michael Quig is the President at Kingspan Light & Ai/ CPI Daylighting and formerly the President and COO of Tredroc Tire Services. He understands the power and value of NCG. We accidentally met in a coffee shop where Mike was meeting with a mutual friend, seeking help with his job transition. We quickly became great friends.

Ed Toczyski is the Vice President at New York Life Insurance Co. and was a quick study of the principles of NCG. We have known each other for more than 20 years. Ed embraces the "G" in NCG and has made a difference in the lives of many young people.

Michael Verden is founder and CEO of The Lake Forest Group, a strategic security consulting firm, but he has an illustrious career as a police officer, twenty-one years in the Secret Service in the Presidential Protective Division and the Counter Assault Team. He has provided security consulting for Fortune 500s and notable sports organizations like the NBA, MLB, and NFL and Paypal, American Express, and Blue Cross Blue Shield. Michael is highly skilled at NCG. We met when I was consulting at his prior company and worked with him informally as a coach as he launched his new company.

Gregg Salkovitch is the Owner and Founder of Right Choice Resources. Gregg is one the best sales recruiters I know and has been employing NCG from the day I met him. Gregg is someone who has always put others before himself.

To this day, he will always ask me if I need help. We were introduced through an acquaintance and I have been his informal mentor and friend.

Megan Wessels is CEO of Powerful Partners, Inc. and is known throughout Chicago as the "fairy godmother of networking." Connecting people is a major part of her work and we have a mutual respect for each other. She calls me "Super Larry." Megan is always thinking about how to help others and is an NCG Master. She understands it, and every time we meet, we both learn something new.

PART I

All About NCG

CHAPTER 1

NCG REVEALED

"You've got to meet Bryan, he's a great guy that can really help you," said my friend.

I had heard this before in networking situations. This time, I was grateful for the introduction, but not too excited. I was working as a Regional Vice President in a publicly-held company that offered human capital solutions. Bryan was an intellectual property lawyer and just didn't sound like the type of person I wanted (or needed!) to meet. But since my friend was so insistent, I reached out to Bryan and set up a 1:1 networking meeting at my office.

He walked into the room and I noticed we were about the same age with the same amount of hair. He had an approachable aura and a friendly face. We shook hands and took our seats in the comfortable, black leather chairs at our office conference table. We launched into the businessman's version of small talk, which is sharing our elevator pitches in greater depth, except I noticed he asked insightful follow-up questions and was a great listener. He also set me at ease in conversation, and it wasn't long before we strayed out of the business realm and into our families, hobbies and other personal interests.

Then as our meeting drew to a close, Bryan turned to me and said something that truly changed my life and rewrote my idea about what networking could be.

"Whenever I meet someone new, I make it my best practice to introduce them to two people they don't know," he said. He was as good as his word, and a few days after our meeting, he introduced me to two people aligned with my industry that were valuable contacts for me.

I was intrigued. I felt like I had just met someone who truly wanted to help me. I realized that he walked into the conference room not only wanting to gain something for himself but to give to me as well. He was demonstrating the NCG Factor in action through this simple act of networking, connecting, and giving.

I would always remember Bryan. Not only was he a nice person, but he was an astute networker, connector, and someone who helped expand my network. He changed the way I thought about networking, connecting, and meeting people in general. In other words, he had changed my life for the better.

****

THE NCG FACTOR

The NCG Factor is a formula that fuses three, major relational concepts we all experience throughout our life: Networking, Connecting and Giving.

Perhaps you've heard of these three terms on their own and can even translate what they may mean in the business world separately. The trick is to practice them simultaneously, to unlock their true, life-changing power. You'll gain access to the people you want to reach but more importantly, you can also actually change the way you are remembered on this earth. Yes, using the NCG Factor makes you memorable because just like having a dose of charisma, it's noticeable when people do or don't have "it."

At the press time of this book, my LinkedIn network is comprised of almost 30,000 people, and many of them remember me best for making an important introduction for them or helping them reach an important goal. Here's one example from Peter K. Braxton.

> *"I had a chance to look back at the connections that Larry has made for me over the years. I have more than 300 emails where his name is mentioned in 2.5 years. Larry does not work in my organization, I see Larry 2-4 times a year and there are 300 emails where he is mentioned in just over 900 days, for an average of once every three days! Over the years, Larry's business intuition and connects have triangulated on spectacular connections that have and will result in clients for the Family Office I work for."*

Still, I wish I had been introduced to the NCG Factor earlier in life because I know I could have helped even more people and expanded my network in the process.

NCG is powerful, as is passing it on. By modeling NCG for me that day he came to my office, Bryan set me on a path to touch countless other people's lives.

"N" FOR NETWORKING

Whether it was in the elevator, a boardroom or sitting in a coffee shop, I'm guessing you've been to a networking event. But what's your definition of networking?

I used to define networking as showing up at a 1:1 networking meeting (not unlike my meeting with Bryan) or attending a general networking event. I would breeze into a room with no real agenda or attend that 1:1 networking meeting without strategy or purpose. At a networking event, I would move from person to person, exchanging information, and never getting past the small talk to learn anything meaningful about them. For me, at that time, it was enough to say hello, gather a business card, and then cross networking off my "to do" list for the week. I was really missing the boat!

What I was doing fit into the standard definition of networking, which goes something like this:

"Networking is the action or process of interacting with others to exchange information and develop professional or social contacts."

If you ask me, that's a very dry, self-serving, and limited idea of what networking should be. My definition of networking is not complete without incorporating the concepts of Connecting and Giving. It would look something like this:

"NETWORKING is the action or process of initiating a relationship to CONNECT them with my circle of influence and knowledge, ask questions and really listen to find out what they need and GIVE back to them and those most important to them."

See the difference? My definition is other-focused.

It leads to relationship-building rather than information exchange. Best of all, because we are building relationships, not just exchanging information, networking isn't confined to designated "networking events" with a coffee cup in hand. It can happen at your child's baseball game, your church picnic or standing in line at the supermarket checkout.

Any time you are speaking with someone, you can be networking and building a relationship. You can learn about them, who they want to know, and how you can help each other. You can find out their goals and if you can help them, whether it's raising funds for a cause, promoting an event, or finding a new job. Peter Braxton agrees with this too.

"Networking is not something that is taught in school. There is no formal education on it until you get to graduate or business school. However, being nice to people and finding connections and things in common is naturally what we do since pre-school! It is important to remember that creating this network takes time and deliberate effort and curation. It's where most of us give up, when we don't see immediate results. Larry has taught an approach to networking that helps reframe what immediate results actually look like, building it one person at a time."

In the typical business networking situation, however, it's important to have an agenda. You should have a reason for being at the networking event you choose to attend. For example, you may want to meet three people in a certain industry or find one person with a certain skill. You can come prepared with names of people you would like to know, companies of interest, etc. if you have a list in advance. If you do not have a list, then you still need to have a goal or action plan to accomplish what you want at that networking event. The more specific and prepared you are for your networking event, the more measurable and impactful your results will be.

If you are having trouble reaching your goal at the event, you may be in the wrong place. When it comes to networking, go for quality not *quantity*. It's not how many people you network with, it's how strategically you do it, so your time is well spent.

As social beings, it's natural to connect face-to-face, usually over a cup of something or a meal. But when it's not practical because of distance or time constraints, you can still network. I've had many successful networking phone calls that have gone far in building relationships. I also have a lot of people in my network who I have never met but have become important contacts for me.

It's important to know how to network. But being a great connector takes networking to the next level.

"C" FOR CONNECTING

The second component of the NCG formula is Connecting, but the art of connecting is second to none! Connecting is the power to bring two people together who can truly enhance each other's lives on a personal and/or professional level. Become a good connector and you will be remembered and beloved.

It's in connecting that we can truly shape or reshape

our legacy. I will always remember Bryan as a great connector because of his valuable introductions. How do people remember you? When you leave this Earth, will they remember how you helped them build life-changing relationships? How you helped them reach their goals?

Connectors show up at networking meetings knowing that something good will come out of it. They are there to help others find what they need. Connectors purposely give of their network resources and their time to make introductions. They also make it known that they are connectors so they can help others.

I do this very overtly at networking meetings. I want people to know what I can do for them. I want them to think of me differently from the other people they met that day, that week, that month, or even that year. So, when it comes time to stand up and give my elevator speech, I also say something along the lines of...

"One thing I want you to know about me is that if you are ever in need of something, I want to be the person that you call. I may know someone who can help you."

A good connector's modus operandi is helping others. They are remembered for the others they bring into someone's life. What if at every networking meeting you ask, "How can I help you or others that you know?" That one sentence can change the outcome of your meeting for you and the other person.

I'll tell you a secret. Before meeting Bryan, I don't think

I had a legacy I could be proud of. It wasn't that I was a bad person; I just hadn't done anything extraordinary for anyone. Using NCG, I have built a vibrant, dynamic network of people who regularly ask me, "Do you know someone who…?" I'm happy to make valuable, meaningful connections to others and best of all, help those in search of the right people. I know I will be remembered as a connector. In many cases, I'll be remembered as a person who changed their lives by introducing them to the right person at the right time.

Megan Wessels is dedicated to creating authentic alliances with like-minded, mission-focused professional women to help them grow professionally and personally.

"Occasionally I receive a message from Larry about someone he's trying to help through a connection. For instance, there was a woman who had applied for a job and the HR director for the company was part of my network. Larry reached out to me and asked if I would mind making an introduction to the HR Director. I was happy to make the connection for someone I didn't know, because Larry asked. This is something that sticks out in my mind when I think of Larry….the fact that he's willing to take the time to look for a connection that could help someone get a job, and then to ask for an introduction. Whenever I get connected to someone who is seeking work, I now take the time to make connections that could help them secure a job."

If you think about it, when we look back in life, we not

only remember the people who have touched us most but also how we met them or how they approached us. If you're that connector, you'll be remembered.

I can almost guarantee you have been in a networking meeting and asked about the other person's family. They may have mentioned that one of their children in college was looking for an internship, but it's been difficult. Most people will respond with empathy and a wish that the daughter find an internship. However, a true connector will ask to meet or speak with their son or daughter and find out more about the internship they are seeking. Confident connectors would declare that they can help the college student land that internship. It's a different thought process and approach for many, but it's the process of being a true connector and a giver.

Being a connector also comes with benefits. When you give, you get. Recently, my son was searching for an entry-level position in his field of interest. Fifteen years ago, I could never have reached out to my relationships to help me with a personal connection because I was not a connector back then, and never took the time to give to others. However, now I have built life-changing relationships that I can leverage to help my family, friends, peers and myself. Recently, I also reached out for help for a relative and was overwhelmed by the response I received, even from those who I did not know as well. Peter Braxton notes...

"A contact or connection is only a bad one if one of the connections is not authentic and genuine. There is no quicker or better way to discover that than by making the connection. You get feedback, both good and bad from a connection and good connections reinforce themselves. More connections are made, the bad and always disingenuous go to the back of the line or are discarded. In this way, the reward of finding authentic and genuine people outweighs the risk of a missed or bad connection."

That's how being a connector works. Like a splice between two wires, your help serves to bring two energies together to light the world more positively than they could ever do on their own.

"G" FOR GIVING

There have been many books written about giving in business situations, and I'm in agreement with every single one of them. Being a giver is an important state of mind for anyone applying the NCG Factor and the reason for the letter "G" in the acronym.

People who understand the NCG factor give of their network by connecting others when the opportunity arises. When someone asks for help, they freely give of their personal talents and resources. In other words, for anyone practicing NCG, giving is intertwined with connecting and giving as a way of life.

Most of us are used to hearing the word "giving"

associated with philanthropy. Philanthropy is great! But while we may not have millions of dollars to give away, we all have been given something to share with the world. It may be a special skill or talent, our access to people or resources, great knowledge, spare time, or a passion for a cause. Whatever it is, we can take it into the world and start helping people! And networking and connecting leads to giving as well.

Giving can become part of who you are and what you do every day. As a producer at one of the largest insurance brokers, Robert J. Kunz has found an innovative way to be a giver:

> *"Within my current role I set up and host events to bring industry professionals together. By gathering a targeted group of people who all have services that benefit one another into one room, on regular intervals, I become the bridge that enables the flow of their business. Through events like this, I expand the network of every single person that attends and create an opportunity to help their business. Once again, by giving first, I am in a position to receive a referral back. Larry's approach has changed me to become a connector and a giver."*

If you are a giver, you shouldn't be afraid to ask, "Can you do me a favor?" Nothing should keep you from asking that simple question. Most of the time people will respond with curiosity. "Sure, what do you need?" If you are a giver, you know deep down that someday you will also be available for that person who does you a favor too. Peter Braxton explains it this way...

"In my opinion, reciprocation is the strongest business emotion behind "fear" and "greed." When you can create value through a connection, both connections feel obligated to return the favor. It is through this obligation, that eventually doesn't feel obligatory, that business connections are made. Over the years, Larry's business intuition and connects have triangulated on spectacular connections that have and will result in clients for the Family Office I work for. I have reciprocated to him and others, and the good cycle repeats, but only for those who believe in the faith and power of making connections and curating a personal brand and network."

Are you a believer, then, in the power of NCG? How can you reciprocate for those who have done great things for you?

PUT IT ALL TOGETHER IT SPELLS NCG

I met Mary similarly to how I met Bryan—through a friend who insisted we get in touch. "She's really entrepreneurial and somebody you should know," he said.

Mary works as a sales and business consultant and facilitates mastermind roundtables of entrepreneurs on a regular basis. This was some years ago when the popular business networking tool, LinkedIn, was just getting started. Right away, LinkedIn became one of my favorite ways to network and communicate and I loved to watch my number of connections grow every day as I accepted connections and sent invitations to professionals across the globe. I was also using it to recruit talent for my clients at the time.

As Mary and I conversed and got to know each other, I told her I had a special interest in LinkedIn and was discovering ways to generate leads and help make connections with others. Since Mary is a master of the NCG Factor, she immediately saw a way she could give and at the same time connect me to this special group.

"How would you like to come to my entrepreneur's group and give a presentation on LinkedIn?" she asked. "I'm sure everyone would like to know a little bit about it and how they can best use it for business."

At that time, I had not done any public speaking anywhere, so at first, I was hesitant. Did I really know more than anyone else? Could I really give value to the audience? Now, I look back on that opportunity as a life-changing moment because not only did my presentation go well, but I realized that I had a special knowledge in this area that I could share with others. I sought out more and more speaking engagements and today, I'm an internationally renowned speaker on the subject of LinkedIn. I can truly trace my speaking career back to the opportunity Mary gave me when she applied her NCG Factor for my benefit. That's what I call a life-changing relationship!

Becoming a master of the NCG Factor takes time and

CHAPTER 1: NCG REVEALED

practice. It's truly a mindset shift from "what can this person do for me?" to "what can I do for this person?"

Whether you adopt the NCG Factor like a pro or you have been the lucky recipient of someone's NCG Factor (as I have), the results are powerful and life-changing. When someone is firing on all three of the NCG cylinders they have great personal power to facilitate amazing things between at least two (initially) but potentially hundreds of people down the road.

The best part is that the NCG Factor principles apply just as well in your personal life as your business. Using NCG in your personal life will benefit friends, family members, and everyone else you meet as you journey through life. The possibilities here are endless. Once you open up your network to your loved ones, you can help them with everything from finding doctors, tutors, ballroom dance partners, future spouses, used furniture, help moving, etc.

Personally, I sleep better at night if I know I have given of myself through a connection or a fruitful networking relationship during the day. The NCG Factor has contributed to rewriting my legacy and helping me be remembered as someone who has changed the lives of others. I couldn't do it without this powerful formula. My guess is you'll sleep better after mastering it too!

But as important as it is to understand when you are using the NCG Factor, it's just as important to recognize when you're not. That's why it's important to know what a "taker" is and how to avoid being one. And that's what we'll discover in Chapter Two.

CHAPTER 2

TAKERS NEVER WIN

It was the classic "show up and throw up."

I sat across from the C-suite executive who was in transition and heard that I was a great connector. It was a two o'clock meeting and he was right on time. We shook hands and sat down across from each other in the coffee shop. It was noisy, but where we were sitting allowed me to filter out the noise and focus on our conversation. My executive had an agenda, and nothing would distract him from it.

At first, I listened and waited for him to bounce back a question. Like when you ask someone where they're from and they ask where you're from. But the question never came.

Soon he launched into a speech about his current situation, the kind of new position he was seeking and why, and eventually he naturally transitioned into some details about his personal life as well. *Would he ask about mine?* I wondered. Nope.

It was two thirty now and he was still going strong. I smiled and nodded, listening as I always do, but it was starting to become a social experiment now. Would he ever ask anything about me? He went on about his leadership philosophies and some of the other places he had interviewed, ignoring the things we had in common.

Fifteen minutes later, it was as if an alarm went off in his head. He looked at the clock and declared he had to leave. He screeched his chair away from the table, rose heartily shook my hand and whisked out of the room. I wondered if he even remembered my name.

I never got the license number of that hit and run taker.

****

How do you know if you're a taker? One way to find out is to learn more about the behavior of takers. Then we can make sure we do not make any of the same mistakes they do.

Takers are not bad people. In many cases, they are just uneducated about the finer points of networking. I believe there are three major types of takers, and you can usually recognize them by how they act and what they say. By knowing what category your taker falls into, you may even be able to help them. Ironically, your taker may help you become more of a giver!

TYPES OF TAKERS
The Innocent Taker

The innocent taker is a person who does not realize that they are a taker or being perceived as a taker. They are not consciously being thoughtless or self-centered in their networking meeting. In fact, they would be surprised to hear it. These people usually fall under one or more of these categories:

1) They are very socially unskilled or not paying attention and they don't read social cues well, or realize that the person across the table has not gotten in a word since the meeting began.

2) They are nervous, and just not realizing how much they are talking.

3) They are desperate and in "gotta find a job" mode, and are so consumed with their need to find employment they are blind to anyone else's needs.

4) They are truly ignorant of what a good networking meeting is supposed to look like and think everything's going well.

The innocent takers are the ones who are most coachable and can even be thankful for your advice. Innocent takers can often be easily converted from takers to givers. I have even coached them "in the moment."

For example, the meeting with the executive at the beginning of this chapter came to an abrupt end. But if it had not, and we would have had more time together, I would have taken the opportunity to give him some coaching and guidance. When he finally wound down from his personal spiel, I would have taken the floor and said:

"Since you're looking for a new job, I know you're going to be meeting with a lot of people. I'd like to give you some advice in your 1:1 networking meetings. With a different approach, you could gain their trust and build a relationship to last a lifetime and potentially help you this time, as well as the next time too. Can I give you some pointers?"

I would go on to sensitively explain to him about takers, how you never want to be perceived as one, and challenge him to try to make the next 1:1 a mutually productive one.

One of the easiest ways to step off on the right foot is with gratitude. They could say something like...

"I'm so glad you could meet with me. (Insert Name) said you are someone who really may be able to help me. But I'm looking forward to finding out a little bit more about your needs too, so I would also like to know how I could help you."

By opening up the meeting this way, you are accomplishing several things in a single interaction. First, the person across the table knows that you are not a taker, and you are someone who is interested in offering help as well as receiving it. Second, you communicate that the meeting will not just be about you, and you are interested in hearing about them as well. Finally, and most importantly, by offering help to them right away, you make it more desirable for them to help you.

Innocent takers will genuinely thank you for this advice. They are looking to improve themselves and be the best they can be in their 1:1 meetings and they want to avoid the label of "taker" at all costs.

THE DEFAULT TAKER

The default taker, as the name implies, is a taker in "default" mode. They will be a giver, but only when asked. Again, they are not bad people or generally selfish. In many cases, they don't think to give. It just doesn't come naturally to them, but they're not averse to it either.

A perfect example is Adam, an attorney I knew in my public accounting days. Adam was competent, wealthy, and a really nice guy. I made a number of strategic connections for him that turned into good clients. He always thanked me for giving him the business, but he never made an introduction for me. After a while, I realized that he was stuck in taker mode, but I had a feeling that because he was such a nice person, he just needed to learn how to give. So I made a plan.

I looked through his LinkedIn clients and picked out ten people I wanted to get to know. Then I took him out to lunch. During our conversation, I mentioned that I took the time to review his network on LinkedIn and I was very impressed. Also, I told him some stood out as people I would like to know. I asked him if we could discuss some of those people to better understand how well he knew them. He agreed and we reviewed all ten people and he replied that he knew them all very well. So then I respectfully asked, "If I drafted an introduction for myself to simplify the introduction process, do you think you would be willing to send it to these ten contacts on my behalf?" Because at heart, Adam was a true giver, he was willing to do it for me. All I had to do was ask. Within 72 hours of receiving my introduction, he sent all ten introductions and one became a client of mine. I was able to convert a Default Taker into a Giver with results. (See Appendix for introduction templates you can use.)

THE TRUE TAKER

The True Taker is crafty and ingenuous when networking, stingy with connections, and doesn't think to give at all. The true taker doesn't do all the talking in a 1:1 or hog the floor. He or she has an agenda and is there to achieve something without you realizing what is happening.

Recently, I had a meeting with a true taker. At the time, I possessed the contacts he desperately needed, and all he could think about during our meeting was getting them out of me. I knew this because as we spoke, most of the questions he asked were about the people I knew. It quickly became apparent to me that his interest in me was purely to get access to the people I knew.

This taker will not appreciate advice because they know exactly what they are doing. If you ask them for introductions or connections, they will probably hem and haw, say they don't know the contact, make excuses for not sharing and leave you empty-handed, even as they hold out their palm for you to give them your contacts. You also will never hear the words, "How can I help you?" out of their mouth because they don't understand the concept of giving. If you ever have the opportunity to point out what you see in their behavior, they may give you a reply like, "I've been doing it this way for twenty years. That's just the way I am."

It's true that givers shouldn't always expect something in return, but on the other hand, you need to be able to identify takers. Why? Because you should not waste your time trying to convert these people. So what do you do with them? Do you do business with them? Or do you eliminate them from your network?

TAKERS IN YOUR NETWORK

Every contact doesn't always turn out to be a life-long relationship but when you are using NCG, they often do. On the other hand, it can get very discouraging to have a network filled with takers because they drain you of your resources and offer nothing in return. When the taker is a really nice person who is excellent at his or her job, or is an important referral source for your network, you may decide to keep the taker in your network on a case-by-case basis.

Takers appear in our personal life too, don't they? They come in the form of a neighbor who is always borrowing things but who disappears when you are in need. Or the friend who calls up only to talk about themselves, never asking you what's going on in your life. Do we cut these people out of our personal lives like we do with takers?

The important thing, in both your business and personal life, is to have a mix of relationships in your base of contacts. If eighty percent of your contacts can be classified as takers, it may be time to reevaluate your network. You don't have to have thirty-thousand LinkedIn contacts; there is no magic number. You could have one hundred or five hundred people in your network, as long as they are quality contacts. The same rule applies to friends. Do you have enough true takers in your network to balance out the innocent, default, and true takers?

For example, Erica may be a true taker, but she's a great CPA and clients love her. She's a good reflection on me when I refer her, but I know I should not expect any referrals from her because she is not a giver. I also should not expect to coach her into being one either, because it is just who she is. And that's ok. As long as I understand who I am dealing with, we can still help each other in the ways we are able to do so. Meanwhile, she is still helping my clients and I am still perceived as a connector by introducing Erica.

But who's to say that by continually sending Erica referrals, or helping grow her business, that she won't learn to give back to others as well? There's hope even for the truest, hardcore taker to become a giver.

On the other hand, takers can also try our patience. We may start to be "courted" by other contacts who show a greater interest in helping our business grow. This may encourage us to find other trusted alliances. We may want to shift out the takers and use vendors, trusted advisors, businesses or partners who send us more referrals and show more interest in us and our work. It's absolutely natural for us to want to work (and play) with people we like and respect.

The same goes for friends in our lives who are takers. The oldest sitcom plot in existence is the boyfriend or girlfriend who uses their significant other for tickets to the big rock concert, a date to a dance, or admission to a special club. We may know and tolerate takers in our lives for one reason or another, but there may come a time when we want to reevaluate the relationship.

When it comes to adding people to my business network, though, I want people who understand the NCG Factor. I want people who know how to give and not expect in return, but also people who I delight in helping because I truly care about them.

LOOKING IN THE MIRROR

It's possible you're reading this chapter and thinking to yourself, "Oh no! I think I'm a taker!" Don't worry, there's no distinguishing marks and nobody need ever know and yes, there is help! You can start doing things differently from now on. In other words, it's never too late to start putting the NCG Factor into place.

You can start by looking back at the people who have been quietly helping you with strategic introductions and new client referrals, such as your mentors, coaches, strategic partners, etc. You have two missions with these people: thank them and give back. It's so powerful to reach out and say thank you with a small, surprise gift or a handwritten note. Never mind that it is belated; it will still be appreciated. And never forget to ask them the sixty-four-thousand-dollar question --what can I do to help you? In your personal life, this pertains to those people who have been good and loving to you, the ones you can call and will always be there for you, and the ones who you have lost touch with, but still respect you.

The sooner you learn the principles of NCG, the sooner you will be able to accelerate your success. However, even if you are introduced to the concepts later in your career, you can still use the NCG Factor to your advantage. It's an all-ages ticket to building life-changing relationships and thriving in your business and personal life.

One of the purposes of this book is to start thinking about the right relationships for you —in both business and your personal life—and the potential for those relationships to turn into life-changing ones. Are you surrounded by takers or givers? Are the people in your life the right people? Are the people in your networking group that you go to every month the right people? There will always be takers who will not change and who will refuse counsel and coaching. There will also be those people who want to be connectors in your life. Do you have the right mix, the right ratio, to thrive in your business and personal life?

Remember, too, that it is vitally important to protect or develop your reputation as a giver, not a taker. If you are known as a taker, chances are you may be one. People talk amongst themselves and before long, takers are exposed for who they have shown themselves to be. They are also soon replaced by people who are more genuine and truly interested in helping others than they are.

If you are a taker, take heart! It's never too late to rewrite your legacy. We can all learn to be a giver, even as we network and connect. And one of the easiest ways to do that is to harness the power of one of the best networking platforms available today—LinkedIn.

CHAPTER 3

THE NCG FACTOR & LINKEDIN

It was 2004 and I received a strange email in my inbox from someone that I hired in a previous company—an invitation to connect to something called LinkedIn. I clicked to accept the invitation to the free account and entered the most basic information about myself. I began sending out invitations and connecting with people I knew and before I knew it, others were reaching out to me with invitations too!

What is LinkedIn? It's the "Business Facebook," a powerful way to connect with others. LinkedIn launched in late 2003 and I was the 1,115,008th person to join in 2004. In 2019, LinkedIn surpassed 600 million members.

Most people find out about LinkedIn for the first time the way I did, through an invitation. I was doing some executive recruiting then, so LinkedIn's colorful, informative, searchable pages of hundreds of thousands of potential placements and clients were a big help to me in finding talent, researching companies, and identifying top prospects.

Like Facebook, everyone can customize their LinkedIn page (called a profile) with a nice photo and information about their professional accomplishments. Like Facebook, the platform is free but for a small investment, you can receive additional features. For most people, however, the free site is adequate and quite valuable.

Unlike a Facebook page, LinkedIn is a professional networking website. It can give employers and prospective clients a good idea of who you are from a college student to a nurse, engineer, CFO, CEO, etc., but your LinkedIn profile is not your resume. However, chronology of your job history and your education on LinkedIn must align with your resume. You should post work samples and presentations you've done. However, it's ok to let a little of your personality out too. You can mention that you're a triathlete, a singer, a scratch golfer, or involved in mission work. That's why LinkedIn is such an interesting networking tool. You can easily find the people who are not only professionally qualified to help you, but ones who also share your same interests.

Everyone can use LinkedIn: the college student seeking an internship as well as the retiree looking to connect with others with shared experiences. It's used by the stay-at-home mom who just launched a blog and the executive seeking a new opportunity. Recruiters regularly search LinkedIn profiles for people in positions similar to the ones they want to fill because LinkedIn puts initial screening information about a candidate's education and experience in the palm of their hands. There is also a special, paid LinkedIn Recruiter membership that is used by independent recruiters and also purchased by corporations for their recruiters and sales-related employees to use. LinkedIn has also developed a paid feature called "InMail," that is similar to email, so recruiters and others with a paid membership can confidentially correspond with a prospect about an open position without compromising their current work situation. LinkedIn can be helpful to everyone, and I have become such a LinkedIn devotee that I have maxed out the amount of contacts—30,000—that I can have on my LinkedIn account!

Today, people use LinkedIn for business networking, recruiting, business development, company research and more. The true goldmine of LinkedIn though, is that by connecting to others, you have access to their network of contacts 24/7/365 if you are a first-degree connection. Yet despite the millions of people on LinkedIn today, I estimate that only eight percent of the population is truly leveraging the power of the platform. I realized this even after years speaking on LinkedIn when I survey audience members at my speaking events. Since my first presentation, I have developed into a sought-after speaker on LinkedIn, a trainer and coach. 2019 marked my eleventh year in that role. As LinkedIn keeps changing and revising their algorithms, I am often called back to give refresher courses so people can continue to stay productive on the powerful platform.

Of course, LinkedIn is an incredible tool for applying the NCG Factor. The more I learned about LinkedIn and became proficient with its features, the better I could apply the NCG Factor to my life. LinkedIn facilitates multiple opportunities for networking, connecting, and giving to others.

NETWORKING WITH LINKEDIN

After I meet someone, receive a business card, or hear them speak, I will most likely send them a LinkedIn invitation. Even if they cannot help me with a specific need at that time, they may in the future. My global network has allowed me to help others whenever and wherever they need me.

LinkedIn differentiates your connections by first, second and third-degree. A first degree is a connection that you have invited, or who has invited you. Usually, you have access to the networks of your first-degree connections, unless your connection has elected to close their network of connections. If you see a connection with a "2nd" at the top right, that person is a second-degree connection, or someone who knows one or more of your first-degree connections. Third-degree connections know one or more of your second-degree connections. Thankfully, LinkedIn helps us by telling us, in the "Highlights" section under a connection's summary section, how many mutual connections we have and what degree connection they are.

Second degree connections are often an overlooked goldmine! Let's say that I connect with John Smith, CEO of ABC Company, who is also a client of mine. John built a network of 500 people, many of whom are fellow CEOs. John is my access point to a second-degree network of 500 people, many of whom are CEOs, who would be good contacts for me. Your first-degree network of connections is the pathway to connecting with your second-degree connections, who are the people they directly know.

Third-degree connections are helpful for information, but harder to reach. However, LinkedIn's INMAIL system, which is a paid feature, can help you reach anyone on the network.

One of the best ways you can use LinkedIn is as a

productive tool to enhance your 1:1 networking meetings. If you are connected to the person you are preparing to meet on LinkedIn (called a first-degree connection) you will usually have access to their network. How is this helpful? You can look through their connections for people you would like to know or consultants and service providers you would like to use.

Perhaps you've had experiences with networking meetings that you've found to be unproductive. After the small talk and the exchange of information about "ideal clients," you may part ways promising to think of others to help your new business connection. The problem is, out of sight, out of mind.

Here's a way of turning the traditional networking meeting upside down using LinkedIn.

Remember when we talked about having a goal in networking situations? Instead of going in without an agenda, I ask people I meet in 1:1 networking meetings to look through my contacts and come with a list of "five to ten" or so people from my network that could help them in some way. I do the same with their network. This intention solidifies the entire NCG formula: a sit-down networking situation, deepening your connection with someone, and giving of your network. 99.9% of the time, people will go through this pre-meeting exercise without hesitation. If they decline, they may not be the referral partner you're looking for.

When you meet, your contact can tell you how well

they know the connections that you have researched and referenced. If they are comfortable, they will not mind introducing you. If in reviewing your lists with one another, if you both come up empty without knowing any of the connections well enough to make an introduction, make a plan to email each other with different lists. This takes a meeting without results and converts it into a meeting with results and action.

If introductions are in order, it is best to write one for your connection, so they don't have to do it themselves. (See Appendix for a sample) This is something I taught to Zori Haouchine.

"During my first meeting with Larry, I learned more about effective networking than all the articles and books I had ever read on the topic. One tip I found particularly helpful was to draft my own introduction to share with those I was requesting make introductions for me. This saved them time and shifted the work of explaining who I am and what I do to me. It made it almost effortless for them to connect me. Another helpful tip was Larry's advice about what to do when I've been introduced to someone who doesn't respond after several follow-ups. He told me to suggest a time and place and send a meeting invite. By taking this initiative, I've been able to get the attention of people who otherwise might have never responded."

I really enjoy coming to any networking meeting with a second-degree connection. I bring a list of our mutual connections, which can be very fun and interesting. You may be surprised to find out that the person you know through business coached little league for your new connection's son. Or your last boss was the second cousin of your new connection's wife! You may also reach out in advance of a networking meeting and contact a shared connection to learn more about the person you are meeting, topics of interest, topics not to discuss, etc.

A word of warning...the "list of five to ten" plan only works when your first-degree connection has their network open. LinkedIn offers the option to keep your network closed, which prevents your first-degree connections from seeing your network. So, should you keep your network open or closed? Many people have asked my opinion on this subject and my answer is usually the same. "What do you want to get out of LinkedIn? Why are you on the platform?" If the answer is to expand your own network by helping others, then you really should keep your network open to be a connector and a giver to others. However, I am always surprised how and why some people choose to keep their network closed.

One day I had a meeting scheduled with an executive and we had agreed to come prepared with our mutual lists of ten connections that we wanted to know. I had already been accepted as a first-degree connection but when I went to his network, it was closed. When I asked him why, he said he feared competitors would see his connections and pursue the same prospects. Instead, he was watching his competitor, and waiting to see who he was connecting with, so he would know their names! He did eventually open up his network for a couple hours at a specified time so I could identify some connections for my list, but his intention in using LinkedIn was clear.

There is no right or wrong to whether you should or should not keep your network open. LinkedIn is your account and network, but remember LinkedIn is a business networking tool. If you are hiding your network and not helping others, you are not engaging the NCG Factor.

CONNECTING WITH LINKEDIN

When I first got on LinkedIn, the "ping" of the notifications of accepted invitations was so exciting. I was amazed at how rapidly my network grew with relatively little tending.

The first step to connecting with someone is to send that important invitation. Your first impression is important. So think of sending that invitation to be as important as stepping through the door at a big job interview.

LinkedIn gives us the opportunity to send a "form letter" invitation or a customized one. I do not respond to the form letter invites because I need to have a reason to connect to that person. So my best advice to you is that if you are sending an invite to someone, remember some simple rules.

- **Make it Personal.** Tell them where you heard their name, met them, or saw them. You can also reference something in their profile you found of interest or in common with your interests.

- **Make it Short.** Get to the point quickly, but be polite, not blunt.
- **Make it Valuable.** Tell them if you have any shared connections, or anything else that is distinctive about you that they would find interesting and would make them want to connect with you.

When sending an invitation on the LinkedIn app on your cell phone, don't just click "connect." It will automatically send a form letter invite. Click on the three dots or the "more" box and choose to customize the invitation. It's one small, extra step but it makes a big difference to the recipient. On the desktop, only connect with someone within their profile headline box and customize the invitation as well. I share these tips with the caveat that LinkedIn is currently in development and these features and steps may be different at the time you read this book.

Connect the right way, and you will begin building a relationship that could become life-changing for you or someone else.

The good and the bad of having LinkedIn is that people you meet expect you to research and know a little bit about them, especially in a job interview situation, but even in a casual 1:1 meeting. After all, they have taken the time to put a LinkedIn profile online. They expect you to read it. Part of connecting is knowing who is in your network. If you are connecting with someone through a meeting, come prepared. It's expected.

Michael Verden, who does a great deal of connecting in his business, puts it this way...

"To be a good connector you need to understand who it is you are meeting with. It's a sound strategy to review the person's LinkedIn profile, especially looking at their employment history, educational background, and connections. You may have some things in common such as the schools you attended or the people you know. Another strategic advantage is to review the company website to learn about their leadership, services, locations, and current news so that you are prepared to have a productive conversation."

GIVING WITH LINKEDIN

Over the years, I have scoured my LinkedIn network to help others find positions from entry level to CEO. Sharing your network provides a wonderful way to give back to others, and there are many ways to do this.

- **Introductions.** As we discussed in the above section, introducing the right two people to each other at the right time can be life-changing for both of them. Just as you may need introductions one day, be sure to be generous giving introductions to help other people.

- **Status Updates.** Like Facebook, LinkedIn gives you

the opportunity to share your expertise in "status updates" that go into the feed of your connections. There is also a blogger platform that you can use to post and to write articles. By sharing your knowledge and expertise with the LinkedIn audience, you can establish yourself as a thought leader and endear yourself to your connections at the same time.

- **Research.** You can use LinkedIn to search for talent that may have certain keywords in their headline or in their profile. For example, a charity I work with was looking to hire someone in a development role and I was able to bring in some leads by searching my LinkedIn network for development talent at nonprofits.

- **Recommendations.** Your LinkedIn profile has a place to give and receive recommendations. This is a great way to give back to those who have helped you along the way. If someone has done a terrific job, let others know about it on their LinkedIn profile.

- **Help People Find Jobs.** LinkedIn is a favorite resource for recruiters and there is a special "Premium" subscription that is helpful to them in researching and reaching out to desirable candidates. You can also source talent through your own research with some commercial search limits for free members. You are also welcome to post an update that your company is hiring interns or for a certain position.

One special way I found to give back to the LinkedIn community was to curate a list of summer internships for college-age students. I developed this resource from the LinkedIn job tab but combined the postings into one link so people who were not familiar with the tab would have the information at their fingertips. Then I shared it with direct emails outside of LinkedIn with my peers whose children were seeking internships. I also posted it for all my connections on LinkedIn. It was an easy thing to do and many people appreciated it.

LINKEDIN BEST PRACTICES

So now that you are ready to delve into LinkedIn, or revisit your neglected profile, here are some best practices to consider as you "up" your LinkedIn game.

- **HEADLINE.** LinkedIn uses your headline in searches and so does Google. Make sure it contains keywords that are descriptive and accurate, whether that is your job title or a description of what type of position you are seeking. How do you want people to see you? You don't have to let it stop at your job title. For example, mine incorporates Global Speaker & Author on LinkedIn| Sales Leader-Mentor| Investor-Advisor-Connector. Repetition of the keywords throughout your profile too will help you come up in a Google search or through a search on LinkedIn. If you want to get creative, just do it in conjunction with something sensible. For example, I knew someone who added "Bacon Enthusiast" to his headline. But he was also a "sales executive;" maybe someday he will get a call from a large, bacon manufacturer for a sales position!

- **PHOTO.** Make it professional and current. Save the vacation photos for Facebook. You shouldn't be in a bathing suit, smoking a cigar, wearing sunglasses and a hat, holding a baby or showing off your dog. What do you look like on the job? That's the photo we want to see. And although we all prefer photos of ourselves from ten years ago, you will be viewed as vain if you walk into a meeting looking unrecognizable from your profile picture.

- **SUMMARY.** Tell LinkedIn what you do but also a little about who you are. Here again, is an opportunity to be appropriately creative. This is also your opportunity to provide credibility for the role you hold today, accomplishments over the years and even something about you personally or on the philanthropic front.

- **EXPERIENCE.** Include all relevant positions. Make sure your input matches what is on your resume. Give as much or as little detail as you would like in order to be found in the proper manner by the proper people.

- **EDUCATION.** LinkedIn makes your alumni affiliations searchable so you may connect with current students as well as alumni from your school. Some people choose to include high school or even grammar school. Your choice.
- **RECOMMENDATIONS.** Many people don't think to write recommendations until they are asked. Think about asking past employers, teachers, co-workers, mentors, peers, supervisors, colleagues, etc. to write a recommendation. As you do this, don't be afraid to give them some suggestions and ideas. Remind them of your work together and your value to each project. They will be happy to include your thoughts in their recommendation. Ideally, four to six recommendations is a good number to have on your profile.
- **PERSONAL.** Is there a personal side to your life? Yes, there is! Include some personal information (i.e., volunteering, a hobby, sports of interest, awards you have won, patents held, books you like to read). This helps others find what they may have in common with you or find interesting about you as well.
- **CONTACT INFO.** Include your website and phone number if you want to encourage people to reach out. Otherwise, leave it off.

LAST WORDS TO THOSE IN COLLEGE, RECENT GRADUATES AND NEAR RETIREMENT

College students and recent grads, listen up! LinkedIn is not just something for your parents. In my day, networking could only be done in person and it was difficult to get to the people you needed to meet. You have an incredible "all access pass" to those you want to know in the business or academic world, all at your fingertips with LinkedIn. I'm jealous because I did not have this at your age. Sure wish I had!

Nowadays, colleges are beginning to teach LinkedIn basics, but a lot can be learned by looking at profiles of people you professionally admire and want to emulate. The sooner you start building a network, the sooner you will be self-reliant in reaching out for internships and first opportunities after graduation. Send invitations to your professors, your peers, successful graduating seniors and parents' friends. Start building your network today!

Chapter 6 is devoted to you with a section of tips and ideas on how to use NCG to build life-changing relationships. It may feel awkward at first, but before long, you will know LinkedIn as well as you know your favorite social media platform!

Now it's your turn, parents. Listen up! You can be a role model to your children by making sure they have a LinkedIn profile and that it is professionally done. Yours should be too! Whether you are re-entering the job market, in transition, or retiring, LinkedIn can help you in your journey.

I refer you to Chapter 7, where I go into detail about how to use LinkedIn for your particular phase in life. LinkedIn is one of the most powerful tools you have for easing into a new situation or exiting an old one, and no matter where we are in our adulthood, we can usually all use a little help there.

Not all connections are created equal. Next, we will discuss how to categorize and maximize the NCG Factor with your contacts as they fall into different realms of influence within your network. We call it your inner and outer circles.

CHAPTER 4

NCG AND YOUR CIRCLES

Imagine yourself in the ocean, stranded on one of those round inner tubes, bouncing up and down with the waves, needing someone...anyone...to give you a helping hand. You take a 360-degree look around you and you see a big ship off in the distance, possibly miles away and your heart sinks. How will they ever see you? Do they even know you're there? Will your paths even cross? And you suddenly feel embarrassed to be in your vulnerable position. What will the crew think? You know it's going to be uncomfortable...but you have no other choice.

So you wait, with reflected and overhead sunlight baking your skin, as you continue paddling with futility towards the shoreline. And then you spot it...a speedboat, piloted by one of your closest friends. You wave enthusiastically. "Hey!" you say. "Over here!" You know they'll tease you, but you also know they care. You'll all laugh at the situation together one day. They see you! "Hold on!" you hear them shout, as they grab a sturdy, rope and prepare to toss it to you to give you a tow. You breathe a sigh of relief. You're rescued! And now this precarious situation is about to turn into a fun ride!

That's how it feels when you know who are in your inner and outer circles when it comes to the NCG Factor.

INNER AND OUTER CIRCLES

Everyone has or will need to build their inner and outer circles when it comes to networking, connecting, and giving. Inner and outer circles are a state of mind and a way of categorizing your network so you understand their interest and ability to help you or others in your network.

The people in your inner circle are represented by the speedboat in the story: they are easily accessible, comfortable and always ready to help you. Your outer circle is like that ship in the distance: helpful when needed, but a little harder to reach and not as comfortable to ask for help. Building and understanding the concept of inner and outer circles is important for knowing how to network strategically.

The people in your inner circle know you well. They understand your situation and you can trust and rely on them to help you, no matter what situation you find yourself in. You may see them often, or once in a while, but the feeling that they know, admire, and respect you is always present in your interactions. If they know you are in need, they will fly to your side to help.

Personally, your inner circle is obviously the people who know, love, and respect you the most. These would include the people in your immediate family, close business peers, and your friends. Like the speedboat, you're not afraid to ask them for help and they will willingly give it because they know and like you. And you know doing so will be comfortable, and maybe even fun because you like them too.

However, your inner circle can include people you do not know socially. It can include advisors who have known you for a long time, such as your attorney, doctor, dentist, or a financial planner. Or it may include people you just recently met, and with whom you have an instant connection. If you begin helping each other religiously, you may find yourself in their inner circle as they take their place in yours.

Everyone's inner circle is composed of different people, but the common thread is that these inner circle people exemplify the life-long relationship. They are the people you will most likely still be speaking with twenty years from now, even if it is only once a year.

If you learn about the NCG factor and commit to using it, your inner circle will begin building before you leave college. Your fraternity/sorority siblings, your professors, your teammates, marching band pals, roommates, etc. can remain in your inner circle, ready to be of assistance when you graduate. The goal throughout life is to get more and more people into your inner circle so you continually expand your life-long relationships.

In terms of LinkedIn, your inner circle is usually comprised of individuals who are first-degree connections. However, they absolutely COULD be second or third-degree connections that are people you know and should be your first-degree connections. If so, make sure you send them an invitation to LinkedIn so they can become first-degree connections! But there may also be plenty of people in either your inner or outer circle who do not use LinkedIn. As we explained in Chapter 1, connections can be found anywhere!

Basically, most of us do not have hundreds of people in our inner circle. We may have as few as five, a dozen, or as many as a hundred. But expanding your inner circle is a good goal and something that will benefit us all.

So, who makes up your outer circle? The outer circle is comprised of people who you don't know quite as well. They may be people you met at a networking event, distant relatives or past acquaintances. You may have known them since birth or just met them. They will most likely help you if you called them with a request, but only if asked, kind of like that far off ship in the example story. In short, they're not quite as readily available and eager to help as the people in your inner circle. It also might be more uncomfortable to ask them for a favor since you don't know them as well, or perhaps you haven't spoken with them in a while. They may vaguely wonder why your request is coming to them instead of someone who knows you better.

Your outer circle is also most likely much larger than your inner circle. We begin building our outer circle when we are young, and it expands rapidly as we meet people at conferences and events, or start work at large, multi-departmental organizations. We expand our outer circle continuously throughout our lives. In fact, I consider a large percentage of my 30,000 contacts in LinkedIn in my outer circle. Your outer circle might also contain people that you would like to be closer to you, either personally or professionally. That's why it's good to know that an individual's "position" in an inner or outer circle is fluid.

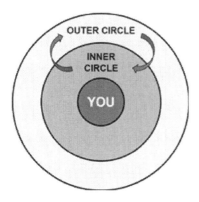

Yes, people in your outer circle can move to your inner, and vice versa. In fact, just think how much good you could do for others if all those outer circle people were suddenly in your inner circle, available to help you. You'd leave quite a legacy! In fact, the trick throughout life is to get as many people from your outer circle into your inner circle. No small feat!

The reasons people move in and out of your inner circle are many, but usually involve an overture of some sort. In other words, someone reaches out to someone else to GET a referral, connection, introduction, or favor. Or, someone reaches out to someone else to GIVE them something, like a referral, connection, or introduction. When the overture happens from someone in your outer circle, it is a sign that they consider you in their inner circle and they are ready to take their place in yours.

As I said, the inner and outer circles are a state of mind, but it's still important to think about people within these places. Why? Because knowing who is in your inner and outer circles will help you determine who would be the best person to contact for a request, whether it is something you need for yourself or for a close family member or friend. If you know who is in your inner circle, you can save a great deal of time searching for an ally because they will immediately come to mind.

Taking a look at your LinkedIn profile and the connections within can help you figure out who is in your inner vs. outer circle. It's a good exercise to do every once in a while, especially if you are reaching your limit on LinkedIn contacts. It's also important to define your inner and outer circle to make your networking as productive and strategic as possible!

WORKING THE CIRCLES

Let's say you've established who is in your inner and outer circle. You now know where to go first if you, or someone you know, is in need.

Whether we are firmly planted in a position in a company or actively seeking a new one, most of us encounter a time in our lives where we are in transition especially for your first job out of college. When that day comes, the best way to find what we need is to reach out to others—in other words, our network of connections. And, if we have defined who is in our inner circle, we know where to start!

I was working with a CEO in the real estate industry whose job was eliminated after the owners of the company decided to sell their portfolio of real estate holdings. He was in his early 50's, had made a comfortable living and still wanted to continue working for several more years. The only problem was that he hadn't concentrated on building a deep inner and outer circle. He had to start from scratch, building up his LinkedIn presence and finding and connecting to the many people whose lives he had touched as a co-worker, supervisor, mentor, and friend over the past several decades. As he started reconnecting with people, he began to mentally determine who was in his inner and outer circle.

To his surprise, he found that some people in his outer circle were more receptive to his cry for help than his inner circle. When that happens, you know your "outer circle" person really belongs on the inside.

Unfortunately, the opposite happens too. I once had a wonderful, giving, working relationship with someone and we regularly fed each other referrals. He was undoubtedly an inner circle connection. Then he was promoted to a CEO position and shortly afterwards, I found myself in transition. When I reached out to him, I never heard back. Later, when I was once again employed, I reached out to him to reconnect and asked why I had never received a response when I could have used his help. His reply was that with the new position, he was just too busy to help me. He had told me by his actions, that he had moved from my inner to outer circle.

The rest of the story is interesting. I was having a 1:1 meeting with another connection. "I have a friend that you might be able to help," he told me. "He's a CEO who is in transition." Guess who it was? Yes, my original inner circle connection who was now in need of networking help. "Will you help him?" asked my new connection, unaware of my history with the former CEO. "Sure," I said. Sometimes it's not easy to share your NCG Factor, but we all know it's the right thing to do. All I knew at that moment is that if he wanted to regain his position in my inner circle, he needed to be the one to initiate a reconnection, and in a spectacular way!

When I meet someone in need of networking help, one of the first questions I ask them is, "How is your network?" What I am asking is how many people they know, where they meet people and if they do any community service or volunteer anywhere. People usually answer one of three ways: "Good," "Ok," or "I don't have a network."

If they reply "Ok" or "Good," my second question to them is, "Who are ten or twenty people in your network (LinkedIn or personal) that might be able to help you?" In other words, I am asking for some names from his/her inner circle. I ask them to write them down and consider reaching out for a 1:1 meeting or phone call in the next few days. People who claim to have a strong, or even mediocre network can find a beginning with a simple list of their top ten inner circle connections.

Then there are those people who say they don't have a network. They may have a small handful of connections on LinkedIn and spend so much of their time working and with family, they don't have a lot of community involvement or volunteerism to feed their networking efforts. They also may have been in a backroom position, head down, for the past thirty years and just have not had the time, need, or interest in networking. Now, it's all new to them.

If you fall into this category, take heart! I find that

often, people who start out with the weakest networks have the potential to quickly become NCG masters. Because of the urgency of their situation, they willingly embrace the concepts of NCG. They may join organizations to give back, but at the same time network and connect with the new people they meet. Even those who don't have the strongest networks can do a good job of putting together their inner and outer circles and begin connecting in a real and targeted way.

Cultivating strong inner and outer circles should be a way of life, not a knee jerk reaction to the loss of a job. Building strong circles not only helps you when you need it but can help others who ask for your help. That's why keeping your circle strong is important, regardless of your professional status. When you start to think of people as part of your inner or outer circles, you begin to see opportunities and allow people to give you opportunities. You begin to reevaluate the people in your life and sometimes what you find will amaze you. People who you never would expect to be able to help you can become your greatest resource of all.

For example, for years I went to Pete, the barber, who spent most of his working hours talking to men as he worked on their hair. It took me a while to think about his life and the people he came in contact with every day. When I started talking to him about a past career transition as I got my trim, it turned out that he had actually cut the hair of many CEOs and other executives for years. Many of them were people I desired to meet. He said he felt comfortable enough with both me and them to arrange an introduction! Up to that point, I had never considered Pete part of my inner circle, but he certainly was.

HELP FOR SAGGING CIRCLES

Our goal in life should be to always have strong, vibrant inner and outer circles, regardless of our situation. But instead, when we find that new opportunity, for example in an internal corporate role, we may begin to get comfortable and avoid networking, or at least no longer consider it a priority. Suddenly our circles start to sag a little as we neglect to add to them or stay connected in a meaningful way. After all, when we no longer need help, it's easy to stop looking for it.

There are many ways to fix your sagging circles, and some will be more attractive than others, depending on your situation, objectives and personal preference. Here are the top ten ways that have worked for me and others to bolster their inner and outer circles.

1. **Attend events.** Search the internet for events, speakers, panel discussions, lunch n' learns, networking happy hours or a breakfast networking meeting. Pay attention to the invites that cross your path and consider their value for your NCG goals.

2. **Volunteer.** Sit on the board of a charity or cause that resonates with you or help out at a fundraiser or drive.

3. **Work LinkedIn.** Review Chapter 3 for some best practices!

4. **Work Your Associations, Groups and Memberships.** If you are in any groups, both personal (like a running club) or professional, reach out to those people who you may not know who share a common interest with you. Start cultivating relationships (or more relationships) with these kindred spirits.

5. **Alumni.** Think about your favorite people from school. Then find them online and connect! This includes teachers as well as students.

6. **Parents and Family Members.** If you are a young person, start thinking of your friend's parents or other family members as possible connections. Look them up online and see if a LinkedIn connection is appropriate.

7. **Professional Service People.** Think about your trusted advisors or other service professionals (your financial advisor, accountant, insurance agent, etc.). These people talk to other people all day long. Chances are, they know someone you would like to know!

8. **Former Work Colleagues.** Reconnect with people you used to work with. This includes people who have left your current company as well as people at companies that you have left behind.

9. **People in Your Role.** Reconnect or ask for

introductions to people in your role (i.e. CEO, CFO, Engineer, Sales Rep, etc.). Someone in the same role you are seeking is receiving calls from recruiters and others hiring for their companies. Let them know you are interested in positions like theirs.

10. **People in your Inner and Outer Circles.** Consider leveraging your inner and outer circles for introductions to the decision makers or someone at your dream employer who could one day get your resume to the right people.

Remember that your inner and outer circles are in a constant state of flux as you meet and grow your connections every day. As such, it's important to know who and where they are so if you're ever stranded in the ocean, you're looking in the right direction for a rescue!

Now that we understand the importance of these circles, we can start learning more from the NCG masters, and how they have taken these principles and found their usefulness in helping to build strong circles and life-long relationships.

On to Chapter 5!

CHAPTER 5

NCG IN ACTION

Imagine yourself as a chemist in a lab with three test tubes marked networking, connecting, and giving. What kind of reaction occurs when you mix them together?

Chemists always have a strategy and a trust and expectation for the outcome of any experiment, and you should too whenever you are networking, connecting and giving. You can create your own custom formula and have confidence and faith that it will result in...

- Relationship building
- Introductions to new clients
- Contributions to your or someone else's important projects
- Community service opportunities
- More resources to call upon
- Help for matters in your personal life
- Help for others in their personal life

Also believe that each of these "reactions" leads to more positive interactions, even though you may never hear about them. Because I asked my contacts to share with me for this chapter, I found out that indeed, NCG leads to exponential magic. Here's a good example from my friend Michael Verden, who tells an amazing story about how my help set off a chain reaction that led to more than he bargained for...

"So Larry introduced me to Mr. X, who was the president of an insurance company. This individual had a stellar background in business and had previously held high level positions for state government before transitioning to the

private sector. The first thing Mr. X asked me was would I be interested in meeting 15 of his professional contacts. After I picked myself off the floor and was able to catch my breath, I collected my thoughts and responded to his question with a well thought out answer—yes! And these were not your run-of-the-mill connections—these were heavyweights in the business world, truly some amazing professionals with extraordinary backgrounds: Partners in law firms representing high net worth individuals, principals in private equity firms, CEOs, Vice Presidents, etc. At this point, you're probably asking yourself what I did with all of these connections? All of these contacts were developed from one person that Larry introduced me to, and we built a professional relationship. I can't even begin to count the number of people I connected with from these 15 introductions, but I can tell you that it was quite a large number.

After meeting with Larry, by the end of the 12 months I had more than 12 new clients and my failure turned into frustration. Why? Because thanks to Larry I had more clients than I could keep up with and had to hire subcontractors just to handle the workload. So maybe the right word, instead of "frustration," should be "elation" because of what Larry's connection techniques did for my business!"

This chapter gives some examples of how NCG plays out in real life. But before you go playing with your NCG chemistry set it's good to have some guidelines to help you put theory into action.

RECOGNIZE YOUR SOCIAL CAPITAL.

My friend Peter Braxton, who works with family offices uses the term "social capital" to quantify the wealth gained from the NCG Factor. In other words, the people you know have value to you and others, just as the people I know may have value to you and others. Peter explains it this way...

"We stratify people immediately when we meet them: "Where are you from?" "Where did you go to school?" "Where do you live?" "What do you do for fun?" All of these questions are designed to stratify people. Humans have a natural instinct to organize people into "buckets," and then determine how best to interact with them. While we do this, we purposefully accumulate the social capital of knowing people. It's hard work, but after a while, the reward is having access to people and solutions at our fingertips.

Larry is a living example of someone with the discipline and attributes to know that social capital is important and expensive. He has accumulated a lot of it and spends it thoughtfully, yet liberally and the returns have been exponential. The mistake most people make, is that if they do not see an immediate "social capital spend," a contact is either mishandled or discarded. What Larry does differently is to see value in every connection. He's incredible at organizing and curating his rolodex of people and is able to make a connection with accuracy and professional value, saving people time and money."

Peter is right in that I seek value in every interaction I have, and you should too. No matter how old or young we are, we all know people that may be able to help someone else. By networking and making a connection, we can give back to someone in need. Working with family offices, NCG is very important to Peter.

> *"I, like Larry, am less than one person away from someone who can professionally perform any task that involves finance and everything it touches, just about anywhere on earth, and have the power, means, and motivation to move these people into action. Looking back, my ability to organize my contacts and connections the way I can was inspired by Larry and the way he treats his own connections."*

Masters of NCG are always aware of their social capital and are generous with it. Invest it well in those you know and the interest will be returned to you ten-fold!

BE A MEMORABLE CONNECTION FOR OTHERS.

I will never forget my first meeting with Megan Wessels back in 2016. When it comes to NCG, we are cut from the same cloth. She was already an incredible connector, but thirsty for even more knowledge and techniques to improve her results. We had an excellent 1:1, exchanged connections, and parted ways.

Later, I received a special delivery. It was a packet of circular stickers emulating the "Superman" logo but with a big "L" in place of the big "S" usually shown in the logo. It was from Megan and in the note she called me "Super Larry." One of the stickers is now on my laptop and you can bet I will never forget her. Since that day, we have helped each other many times over. Megan recalls..

"A local business owner was looking for a speaker on LinkedIn and Larry wasn't available so he connected us. We met and as I listened to her share an overview about the service her company provides, I realized she could fill a need I had in my company. Her company now provides the bookkeeping for my business. In addition, I was a speaker for her event in 2017 and gained two new clients from it. She has also become a client of mine by attending several of my Powerful Partners Dinner Parties. Best of all, she and her husband have become dear friends and she continues to make amazing connections for me."

You can see how connecting people can result in even more magic. I also went on to introduce Megan to business coaches and other people who provided expert mentorship for her. To this day, she is grateful for the introductions.

My story with Megan gives an example of how you can make yourself memorable, but also how making one introduction can lead to so much more for so many people.

EMPLOY NCG FOR LIFE, NOT JUST WORK

When I was in transition myself, I found that some of my connections I knew the least were the first to give. That's why I have the personal goal of helping one person a week in transition. It's my way of paying it forward.

At the same time, I'm not afraid to ask people for help when I need it, even in my personal life. And I have no problem helping others who have a need in their own personal life. I'm keenly aware of the power of the question, "Can you do me a favor?" Typically, people do not answer that question with a "no." The answer is usually, "What do you need?" followed by either a "yes" or a polite decline. It's perfectly fine to ask for things, just make sure you give back to others, so you are justified in asking and expecting others to help you. When you do that, you will be rewarded along the way as I was, myself, by a friend and peer of mine, former Chicago Bear, Desmond Clark.

Most people know Dez from his days as number 88 for the Chicago Bears. We connected at a philanthropic event for his own foundation. He remembers the early days transitioning from professional football to financial services...

"Professionally, Larry has connected me to those who have directly or indirectly lead to client acquisition for my financial companies. Most importantly, Larry's introductions have truly enriched my life because of the network he has helped me build. There is limitless opportunity to serve and have others serve me in helping me continue to build."

A few years into our relationship, I asked him for a personal favor for my son. Matt is a huge hockey fan and had received a lot of experience in video production during high school and through some part-time jobs. His dream, however, was to work in sports, particularly in his favorite sport, hockey. However, he had also had a rough time in school, being the victim of bullying. I knew that making contact with someone, anyone, from the Blackhawks organization would be an amazing, life-changing experience for him. I reached out to Dez for help.

I didn't know what to expect from him but without reservation, he agreed to help and ultimately connected me with someone from the Blackhawks who invited us to a meet and greet at one of the drafts. There, we were pulled away from the crowd and into a private area where we waited, not knowing who would come through the door. It was Patrick Kane and Jonathan Toews! Meeting players he admired and respected on the ice and off the ice was so uplifting and life-changing for him. The simple, kind act of giving that Dez gave me strengthened our relationship and in my mind, made him an unforgettable giver.

Helping someone in their "real life" feels just as good as doing something for them for their "work life." I had the privilege of doing both for Lesly Marban.

"When I started my own management consulting company, Larry immediately introduced me to several

key people that he believed would be great contacts and potential clients for me. Those introductions have led to other meetings with key people I would have never met if it weren't for Larry.

Larry also knows I have a son with Autism Spectrum Disorder. I had told him I was in search of resources that would build his skills as he grew older that would be necessary for him to be independent and ultimately, find a job. Without hesitation, Larry connected and introduced me to the Executive Director of an autism foundation. I immediately reached out to her to learn more and was so impressed, I joined their Board of Directors. For me, it was a perfect way to help move their mission forward in helping other families who were in the same boat we were in. I don't think I would have found this foundation without Larry's help.

Larry can connect the dots to identify exactly the right contact to put you in touch with. However, what makes him stand out is that he genuinely cares about the people he connects and is always willing to help by putting you in touch with someone you need in your life. Larry has helped me see that the connections you provide to others will multiply exponentially for them, just as his introductions have done for me."

When you make a difference not only in someone's professional life but in their personal life, it takes your relationship to the next level. When you ask someone, "what can I do for you?" remind them that you mean in their personal life as well.

BE STRATEGIC ABOUT NCG

In the first chapter of this book, I discussed the importance of attending networking meetings with a specific goal in mind. I consider it a gift when I have a 1:1 meeting with someone who is very focused and strategic about who they want to connect with and why. I found such a person in Zori Haouchine.

Once again, I met her at the urging of a mutual acquaintance who told me, "I know someone you really should meet!" Originally from Bulgaria, Zori was launching her design and architecture firm and when we first met, I was struck by her eagerness to listen, learn, and apply the NCG principles to take her business to the next level. She recalls...

"Larry has opened doors for me and transformed the way I network. Through example, he has taught me a more selfless, natural way of connecting with people. It's so common to approach networking meetings like a transaction – by thinking about what I can get from the other person and what I can give to them. Now, I focus on getting to know the person sitting across the table from me, which establishes a more authentic connection and generates even better ideas about how we might support each other. Larry's quick wit and willingness to help me without asking for anything in return has taught me that networking can become much more than a transaction. It can become a friendship."

Zori also instinctively embraced the idea of networking strategically, pinpointing exactly who she needed to know, and helping me identify the people she specifically wanted to meet in my network.

"Connecting for connection-sake is just busy work, something few of us can afford in our hectic lives. Being strategic about how we connect people always leads to more valuable connections and is more respectful of everyone's time and energy. Larry has helped me become more strategic about how I network. I am more selective about who I meet with and who I connect within my network. This requires investing time in learning about the people I meet to understand who they are, what they need, and who will be valuable for them to meet.

He has taught me that putting others first and going out of my way to help them will make me a better businessperson. I find people often respond with the same level of generosity and kindness, which makes the world feel friendlier and more communal. Larry also makes me laugh, which I greatly appreciate."

On a personal note, Zori was one of the first people to tell me that I should write a book. You never know what kind of inspiration will come out of your NCG activities!

PROVIDE THE KNOWLEDGE TO PASS ON

In this book I have mentioned "building a legacy" or "rewriting your legacy." We all want to be remembered fondly once we leave this earth. One of the reasons I am so eager to help people is because I want to be remembered as a giver who helped them network and connect. In other words, I want to be remembered as an NCG master.

Although I'm an international speaker on LinkedIn, my greatest joy is teaching and leading by example. Many of the wonderful people in my inner circle that I have interviewed for this chapter have told me that they take what they have learned and pass it on in wonderful ways to others. This makes my day. Like what Steve Kosmalski shared with me...

"In my very first discussion with Larry around some of the challenges I was facing, the first thing out of his mouth was, " how can I help you?" quickly followed by some suggestions. I was taken aback by his willingness to help on our very first interface at a business function! I've tried to take his lead since then, offering help via any connections I may have. As is typical in almost any case of giving, it comes back to you in spades."

Don Hyun Kiolbassa also appreciates my style of NCG.

"Larry is a true inspiration. He has taught me to pay it forward. The best business is built off of relationships. Larry is a giver, and this makes you want to do business with him. He knows how to connect the right compatible people to build relationships."

Michael Quig observes how powerful NCG can be after watching me do it.

"After seeing how Larry connected me with so many key business people in the Chicago area, I tried to start doing the same thing. My network was much smaller than Larry's, but it was still extremely rewarding to help someone I know connect with a job opportunity, executive search consultant, or business deal. Larry's approach to giving and connecting is the gold standard I try to follow today."

What's even more fun is when I see how the techniques I've modeled have gone on to make a measurable difference in not just one connection's life, but others as well. As you go forth in the world, practicing the art of NCG, remember that your actions can affect more people's lives than you'll ever know. Just have faith and confidence that every act of giving is a positive one with positive effects. And who doesn't want to leave that kind of legacy?

Now it's time to learn more about how to apply NCG to your particular situation whether that may be as a student, or someone in search of their first professional position (Chapter 6), someone in mid-career transition (Chapter 7) or someone facing retirement (Chapter 8).

Wherever you are in your NCG journey, I wish you all the best in applying these principles to your professional and personal life. And if my advice has helped you, spread the word about The NCG Factor!

PART II

NCG in College to Retirement

CHAPTER 6

NCG IN COLLEGE

I've said it before, and I'll say it again...you are so lucky to live in the electronic age.

Back in "my day," job hunting was literally pounding the pavement, picking out the right letterhead for the resume, cold calling businesses until my fingers turned blue and stamping and mailing hundreds of resumes to people I didn't know. In fact, I didn't even know if they were still at the company.

You are spared all of that, thanks to the internet, but you also have the additional challenge of increased competition. Now, everyone can find almost anyone they want through the internet. How will you make yourself stand out from the crowd? And how can NCG help you in college and beyond? Let's find out.

DECONSTRUCTING NCG

Depending on your major or course of study, you may have some idea of what networking is. Maybe you think that in the career you are pursuing, networking is very commonplace and necessary for success. Or maybe you think networking is not important at all in the field you are pursuing and maybe even...a waste of time.

Believe me when I say, NETWORKING IS IMPORTANT FOR EVERYONE IN EVERY CAREER. Everyone's lives can be enhanced by networking strategically and with purpose. Furthermore, I believe everyone can benefit from networking as early as your freshman year in college.

Now remember that my definition from Chapter 1 is a little different than the standard one. I changed it up a bit. Let's review.

STANDARD DEFINITION:

"Networking is the action or process of interacting with others to exchange information and develop professional or social contacts."

MY DEFINITION:

"NETWORKING is the action or process of initiating a relationship to CONNECT them with my circle of influence and knowledge, ask questions and really listen to find out what they need and GIVE back to them and those most important to them."

Remember the focus? It's on the other person. By focusing on the other person, you will not only create a connection but begin to build a relationship—possibly even a powerful, transformative life-changing relationship.

Just a reminder too that networking that leads to life-changing relationships often occurs outside of the formal coffee and donuts or luncheon. Currently, you are most likely surrounded by classmates with similar interests and career aspirations. Did you ever think that you could network with them now, for the future?

Perhaps you think you're too young or inexperienced to be of networking value to anyone, or to give or even operate with a "giving" mindset. But you may already be doing it on a daily basis.

For example, if you're a biology guru and your roommate is struggling, what do you think would happen if you offered your help? At the very least you will build and improve your relationship with your roommate for the rest of the semester. But what if your tutoring saved your roommate from certain failure, allowed them to keep their scholarship, and remain at school? Now your good deed becomes a life-changing experience for your roommate, and you will forever be remembered as a giver. Someday, when your roommate discovers the NCG Factor (perhaps even as you pass this book on to them!), they may use it to help you in the future, i.e. help you find a position at their firm, introduce you to your future spouse, or help you buy your first home.

Remember that your classmates will not always be your classmates. Who knows where the future will lead them? Even if they are not part of your inner circle, you can always stay connected to them on LinkedIn or other social media.

If I could go back in time, I would have spent time getting to know the Dean, my Professors and other key faculty members. Many of those professors were published authors, keynote speakers, retired executives or industry professionals who have left their careers to serve their passion for teaching the next generation of engineers, accountants, human resource professionals, etc. Research your professors on LinkedIn and across the internet, follow them, connect with them on social media and stay connected, even if it is only through your posts. Someday we will no longer be their students but possible professional colleagues. Wouldn't it be nice to have an established relationship with them so you may help them find interns, or they can recommend new grads or share new research with you? Have you considered asking one of your professors for a fifteen or thirty-minute mentoring meeting each month or quarterly? You may be surprised how few students do this, and you may also be surprised to see how willing professors are to share their advice and connections to help the younger generation succeed. Let them know your plans for the future and your dream job. They could be your reference for a future job or the connector to a hiring manager for your internship or first job out of college. They could even become the mentor that evolves into a life-changing relationship for you.

I was meeting with a very successful executive that sold his company for 400 Million Dollars. We were discussing a mutual contact we both knew, and he said he was the mentor to his son. I asked him how he became his mentor. He said that my connection's son was dating his daughter while they were in college and they made a strong professional connection. He decided to become his mentor. His daughter broke up with this young man, but to this day both are still in touch.

MAXIMIZING NCG IN COLLEGE AND BEYOND

Let me tell you the tale of two college students. Both

of them are seniors who will be graduating soon, and both are business majors. They both have had internships, and they both have memberships in student chapters of national organizations. Both have excellent grade point averages. Neither of them comes from an immediate family that owns a business or has been successful in the business world. In other words, they have to make things happen on their own.

Now it's time for both of them to graduate and find a job. Let's see their strategies.

GEORGE has some job experience from his internship but has not kept in touch with anyone there. He does not have a LinkedIn profile or any professional social media outlet. His plan is to apply at the internship site, and also watch job boards like Careerbuilder.com or Indeed.com and apply where he can. He also asked his parents if they know anyone who might be able to help him, but because of their career fields, they cannot help much. He has a full-time summer job as a counselor so he will devote what extra time he has to his job search and hopefully be ready in the fall.

MARIE had an internship similar to George's experience. She also has a LinkedIn profile that includes a nice picture and a summary of her skills and her ultimate career goal. Her LinkedIn headline says, "Recent Graduate Seeking Position in Business Development." After leaving the internship, she connected on LinkedIn with all her former co-workers. When someone came and spoke at the student chapter association, she also sent LinkedIn invitations to them. She followed their posts, read the books they recommended, and viewed their speeches on YouTube. She knows what is important to them. She decided to reach out to each of them individually with a personal comment about something they had revealed in LinkedIn, like their new position or an event they just attended.

She recently let them know she will be graduating and is seeking a position. She asked them if they happened to know anyone with an open entry level position. She also has spent the past few years making friends at her part-time job, and has connected with those employees on LinkedIn, as well as all of her professors at the university. She also connected on LinkedIn with her extended family and friends. Finally, she gets a message from someone who was referred to her by one of the speakers she saw at an association conference and had kept in touch with through LinkedIn. He tells her their organization regularly hires new graduates into their sales training program and requests her resume.

If she gets the job, she will connect to the HR professional on LinkedIn. If she doesn't get the job, she will still connect to the HR professional on LinkedIn. That's because while she may not be perfect for the job she wanted today, she may be better qualified and a perfect fit for the company later on.

The moral of the example is obvious. College is the perfect time to begin building your professional network. During your quest to enter the professional world, you should keep building your network. But know that the most important social media for your job hunting efforts is the one your prospective employer is using. While there are exceptions, and connections can absolutely be made on places like Twitter and YouTube, for the most part, people in the business world are looking at LinkedIn.

Looking for ideas on how to create a profile? Nowadays, colleges are beginning to teach LinkedIn basics, but a lot can be learned by looking at profiles of people you professionally admire and want to emulate. Search the profiles of professionals you want to be! This alone will motivate you to put your profile together ASAP. So take a hard, honest look at your LinkedIn or other internet profiles and pages. Be sure to review Chapter 3 for best practices to boost any profile's performance. If you can't be found on the internet for your professional aspirations and accomplishments, what are you waiting for? Start building a profile!

Now you may argue that you are in a creative field, and it is more important to have a blog, a website or an electronic portfolio. Sure, but know that the more places you have to be found on the internet, the more places you have to cross reference your portfolio or creative work. For example, as of the writing of this book, LinkedIn has more than 600 million people using LinkedIn. Building a virtual network there would allow you to be searched for by keywords like "artist" or "writer" and you still connect your online portfolio. Do you think more people would land on your portfolio from a straight Google search?

If you still feel hesitant about the importance of NCG, consider the many good things that can happen once you start! And so much can be done virtually.

- You can connect with those in your life you may want to contact in the future
- You can stay in touch with those you have impressed in the past
- You can learn and grow from those you have met and want to emulate by keeping abreast of their achievements and career moves
- You can offer help to others when you hear they are looking for help
- You can gain access (through online messaging, attending their events, or commenting on their posts) to desirable people
- Your public profile allows desirable people to have access to you
- You can send thank you messages and if applicable, questions through messaging apps
- You can post photos and updates of your academic and professional achievements
- You can possibly write articles that can be shared across LinkedIn and other platforms
- You can give back by writing recommendations or endorsing valued professors and insightful speakers
- You can join groups of like-minded individuals and

engage in discussions
- You can expand your inner and outer circles (see Chapter 4) and begin employing NCG (Chapter 5)

CHAPTER 7

NCG IN JOB TRANSITION

Life isn't a fairy tale. Nowadays it's the rare person who lives "happily ever after" in the same job for thirty years.

Statistics vary, but some say people change jobs up to twelve times in their lifetime and change actual careers anywhere from three to five times in a lifetime. That's a lot of change and a lot of transition for anyone, not to mention fear, despair, anxiety and emotional rollercoaster rides. Good thing we have the NCG Factor to help us through it all!

People in transition are making a change from company to company, job to job, or from one career to another. They may also be someone entering the job market after an absence, like a stay-at-home-mom, a graduating senior from college, a new member of the workforce with experience, like an immigrant, or someone leaving the workforce to work on a dedicated project. They also may be members of the workforce moving from one city to another and need help. That's how I met Gregg Salkovitch...

"I relocated from Cleveland to Chicago and didn't know very many people. I took a job that I loved and was crushing my quota. After being there for almost four years, I was making more money than I ever had in my life. I purchased a condo and life was good. Suddenly, the company decided they were going to sell and laid a bunch of us off.

I was pretty much lost and didn't know what I was going to do. To make matters worse, I had a non-compete so I couldn't even stay in the same industry.

I met somebody through networking who said, "I'm going to introduce you to the best guy who is the most well networked person in Chicago," and he introduced me to Larry. We had a phone call and I shared my story. Larry ended up introducing me to a gentleman that just started a new company and he was the only employee.

I was very skeptical but took the introduction, which ended up changing my life. I went into business with this gentleman and we worked together for six years, growing the company from just the two of us to over 50 employees before starting my own recruiting company.

Without Larry's introduction, none of this would've happened. The most amazing thing to me is that I was a stranger to him. Even though I had nothing to give back to him, he saw that I needed help and went out of his way for me."

Gregg's story illustrates that when we approach someone as a giver, we can do more for someone in transition than we would ever think possible. We'll hear more from Gregg's story later but first, let's explore the ways people are in transition and some best practices for using NCG in each situation.

CONDITIONS OF TRANSITION

Most people who find themselves in transition embody one of two general conditions:

The transition was abrupt. In this situation, the individual was employed and laid off or fired without warning, without any kind of severance package. Unfortunately, oftentimes this individual is the sole breadwinner, and the job was his or her only source of income. In these cases, the situation is very stressful and urgent as the transitory individual starts to wonder how they'll pay the mortgage, pay their kid's tuition, etc. This is the type of situation we all hope to avoid. Occasionally, someone is immediately removed from the workforce for health or safety reasons, but still, people in abrupt transition are usually victims of their circumstances. Then there's the other type of transition...

The transition is planned. In these cases, the individual had some advance notice about their job being eliminated, and they have had an opportunity to prepare for it. Or, their resignation was premeditated, spurred on by a change in leadership or culture, with full knowledge that there was no job lined up to begin anytime soon. Still, their transition is not as urgent. They may live in a dual income household and have a little money set aside to offset their income loss for a period of weeks, months, or even years. These individuals often have the luxury of exploring their options to find the perfect next step. They may even entertain the idea of opening their own business.

When I meet with someone in transition, I tend to ask a few basic questions. They are also questions that the individual him/herself has considered at that point.

Where do you sit financially? This tells me if their transition is abrupt or planned, and if they need a job tomorrow, a few weeks from now or they will be in good shape for several months.

How's your network? Most people answer this question one of two ways....

"My network is good." Congratulations! You have something to build on. Inside your network, chances are your dream job awaits. In fact, most likely your network contains some amazing, life-changing relationships. Next, I ask them about their inner and outer circles (Chapter 4). If they have an inner circle, I tell them that now is the time to contact those people who like, respect, and would do anything for them at any time. Another group to contact is those who they have helped in some way. I tell them to look at their contacts and see if they know anyone who could make an introduction to someone at a desirable company. People you have helped in the past will surely want to give back!

The appendix in the back of this book provides some proven templates you can use to introduce yourself or ask others to introduce you. Now is the time to leverage your network and put them to work for you, as they are willing.

But sometimes I get the reply...

"I haven't had the time to build a network." If this sounds like you, thank goodness you've found this book. Also, know that you are not alone. There are many people with your level of age and experience that do not have a network, or more than a handful of LinkedIn contacts. Usually these individuals are more seasoned and unaccustomed to connecting online, or they have been on a career path where networking is not the norm. Most likely, they have been in a job for many years and have never thought about their next move or who could help get them there.

Remember, it's never too late to build a network of life-changing relationships but you must begin today. Review Chapter 4 for some advice on how to build your inner and outer circles. Begin aggressively applying the NCG principles throughout LinkedIn and all of your online communication so you can begin to build life-changing relationships. You can also build your network by doing the following:

Send transition update emails and make phone calls – "Out of Sight, Out of Mind." I'm sure you have received those email updates from your inner and outer circles about their transition. It's time to construct and send your transition email update to your network of relationships. If you met with five new people one week, most likely after each meeting, even with your inner circle, you may be forgotten or "out of sight, out of mind." It's important not only to send that first transition email but to send it out routinely. I would suggest once every few weeks to be top of mind with your inner and outer circles. In addition, make phone calls to reinforce those emails with some of your closest inner circle relationships. It adds a personal touch and may yield immediate results. (Refer to the Appendix for email template examples).

Build—don't burn—bridges. If you have good relationships at work that remained healthy and intact after your departure, be sure to link to them on LinkedIn or stay connected somehow. They may regularly speak with others in the industry who may know of a position for you and would like to help you.

Attend networking events. As stated previously in this book, you must do this strategically. Looking for a job can be full-time work and your time is at a premium especially if you are still employed and must search in stealth mode. Research and find the events that are liable to be the most fruitful for you and take the time to attend them. As outlined in Chapter 1, be sure to have a goal for your networking and always remember to be a giver!

Meet with people in your role or future role. If you are a CFO, then meet with other CFOs. If you meet with a CFO who is happy in their role but from the same industry, they are undoubtedly receiving calls and emails about jobs you may not know about. Make sure you work through your inner and outer circles, LinkedIn, etc. to request introductions to those CFOs you identify through your research.

It's not what you know, it's who you know. It would be utopia if you could apply to a job opening online and be selected among hundreds of applicants as the perfect candidate. However, relationships can make the difference. In most situations, securing the right job is competitive, so it often becomes more of who you know, not entirely what you know. If you have met all job requisites and also receive a warm introduction to a hiring executive, CEO or Board

Member through your inner or outer circle of relationships, you can secure a competitive edge for that position of interest.

Strike the right balance with the recruiter. When you are in transition, you should look at every option and that includes using a recruiter in addition to anything you can accomplish on your own with the NCG Factor. Recruiters can virtually place your resume right in the hands of those who need to see it. However, you should also be checking your network for inner or even outer circle connections who can do the same.

Another piece of advice I always give about recruiters is to remember that they are people too. Add them to your network. Today they are helping you find a job, but if you remember to apply the NCG Factor to your relationship with your recruiter, you can develop a relationship for the long-term. That way, if you ever find yourself in transition again, the recruiter will know you and set you apart from the other candidates. Do you share connections in common? Or is there something online about the recruiter you may also have in common or can reference during your next conversation? This research demonstrates that you are a strong candidate that took the time to conduct research and build rapport and a relationship. That could advance you in front of their other candidates interviewing for the same role.

Recruiters also may have access to other resources you may need like helping you with outreach to a charity in need of certain industry representatives. Let your recruiter find you a job, but remember that you can give back to them as well. You can offer them a look at your contacts to see if you know any potential candidates for their open positions.

Give Back. When you think about it, being in transition is a great time to think about giving back to not only others, but the community as well. You may have more time, less responsibility, and you have a definite need to expand your network and meet more people. Perhaps it's a rare opportunity to get involved in a cause, charity, or organization that has interested you from afar. Now is the time to be a "joiner." Follow your heart with this. You will meet people like yourself who could truly become life-long relationships for you and may even be able to assist you in your transition right now.

1:1 MEETINGS WHEN YOU ARE IN TRANSITION

When you're in transition, the 1:1 becomes vitally important, but it also has to be done well.

Attending a 1:1 meeting holds special challenges for the individual in transition. If your need is urgent and all you can think about is making that next house payment, you may unconsciously sabotage your 1:1 meeting by coming off as too desperate. You may even come off as a taker (see Chapter 2), which would be detrimental to your goals. This is understandable as your need is great. But it is all the more reason that if you are fortunate to secure a 1:1 meeting with someone who can help you connect with others, you must bring the NCG principles into the meeting with you!

You may ask yourself, how can I be a giver when I am so in need myself? You may feel like the starving man giving away his last crumb of bread. In this situation, it is not the immediate action of giving that is important, but the mindset. Place it front and center.

For example, imagine you are out of work and worrying about paying the bills. Then I set up an important 1:1 meeting for you with Mr. Johnson, who could easily introduce you to your next, perfect employer. If you approach the meeting like a taker (see Chapter 2), Mr. Johnson will be less likely to want to help you. Now imagine greeting Mr. Johnson, shaking his hand firmly and saying the following at the onset of your meeting...

"Hi Mr. Johnson, I'm so grateful to Larry for introducing us. I'm in transition and looking for my next position, but I'm also here to get to know you too and I would like to know how I can help you."

I guarantee you that the meeting dynamic will change and lead to a better outcome for you both. Now Mr. Johnson knows you are a giver, even though at this point you are not in a position to give. Expectations become clear. Mr. Johnson knows you have an immediate need and that you are not in a position to do much for him at the moment but will in the future. With clarity brought to the situation in a respectful, humble way, Mr. Johnson will undoubtedly be more likely to want to help you and to do so as soon as he can. Who knows what kindness you may be able to show Mr. Johnson in the future? Look what happened to Gregg....

"A woman reached out to me and I could tell she was desperate. She was a single mother who just got laid off from her job and had a mortgage. Unfortunately, I didn't have any positions for her and was working about 90 hours per week. What immediately popped into my head was, 'Like her, I've been laid off before and have felt that level of desperation. Larry Kaufman, a complete stranger, helped me and I'm going to pay it forward and help her.'

I spent hours helping her revise her resume, made introductions, contacted firms that are technically my competitors and asked if they could help her. I emailed with her almost every day giving her advice. I invested a huge amount of time to help her and expected nothing in return. She eventually ended up finding a job.

Several years later, I was trying to get into a Fortune 500 account, and I was having no luck. I saw that she happened to have worked there in the past, so I sent her a short note asking for advice. She wrote back, 'I never forgot what you did for me, so I'm going to make an introduction to the decision maker for you.'

Less than 30 days later, the contract was signed, and it became my highest revenue producing account. That's the NCG principle in action. The kindness and giving you show today can come back to you tenfold!"

PREPARING FOR THE 1:1

Whether you're employed or in transition, everyone's time is valuable. That's why when I am meeting with someone, either for networking or specifically to help them in transition, I have a few steps that I take in preparation for our meeting. Not surprisingly, these steps are also helpful for the person in transition to do from their own perspective before they go into a 1:1 transition meeting.

To illustrate how 1:1 preparation is done, let's take the example of meeting with Christopher Smith. Here are some steps I take prior to meeting with Christopher.

1. **Research the Individual.** The first thing I do is take a look at Christopher's LinkedIn profile. I look for anything that we may have in common, like a shared charity interest, employer, or school. I also take note of the same potential similarities based on Christopher's personal summary statement.

2. **Research related connections.** If they are a second-degree connection, I find the warmest mutual connection or connections we have, and I reach out to that person or to other mutual connections to find out how they know Christopher. Not only is this a great way to gather more information for the meeting but it's also a great way to renew my relationship with that connection!

3. **Research the company.** I will also research the company where Christopher works/worked. I will then check my connections to see if there is anyone that I know who has worked at the company before, maybe even in the same or a similar role. I may send a message or give them a call to find out a little about the company history. Maybe I'll discover that they are an excellent employer, or that they are always in turmoil. Either way, I come into my meeting with Christopher with some insight into his current or prior work experience.

4. **Send an invitation to connect.** You can send a customized invitation prior to your meeting or post meeting.

Regardless of the situation, taking time for research and due diligence prior to meeting with someone will always make you feel more prepared and relaxed when you enter the meeting, whether it is a job interview or a 1:1 networking meeting. Adopt my system or customize your own, but have a process for making these meetings as productive as possible. Doing so will reflect well on you, your professionalism, and your potential to be an excellent candidate for any position!

ATTITUDE CHECK

How do you feel about being in transition? Angry? Betrayed? Or excited to enter a new chapter in your life?

There's no doubt about it. Being in transition can make

anyone nervous, stressed-out, discouraged, depressed or just plain irritable. You might feel like someone running around a track, nearing dehydration, without a water station in sight! A run of unsuccessful job interviews or attendance at networking meetings with people who do not seem helpful at all can make anyone lose hope. So, what can you do?

First, it's important to keep the ultimate goal, whatever that is for you, in mind. Concentrate on expanding your network. If you do not know who to talk to, someone else might. Make your intentions known to people you meet, but don't forget the "G" in NCG. It can lift your spirits and help you keep a better attitude during your search.

Keeping the mindset of being a "giver" is a great way to keep your spirits up. Seek to give. As mentioned above, now is the time to be a "joiner," give back to the community and in the process, expand your network of like-minded people. It's hard to be sad when you've just helped someone achieve something and they are brimming with joy and gratitude for having you in their life! This is the goal with NCG.

You can also think of your transitional period as a time to take stock in what you have done and what you want to do. If you are a little on the older side, you can even start thinking about your legacy after you're gone. How will you be remembered? As a dedicated volunteer? A devoted family man/woman? A giver? A taker? Or someone who was successful in business and nothing more?

Allow your transition period to be a time to pivot your

priorities, at least temporarily. Doing something new may break you out of your routine and change your perspective on life, not to mention the opportunities you may discover to grow personally and professionally.

NCG is your friend in transition. Buckle it in next to you for the roller coaster ride you may take to find your next opportunity. You can climb hills and speed down them together, but when you finally reach the station, the perfect, new opportunity will be right there waiting for you.

CHAPTER 8

ARRIVING AT RETIREMENT WITH NCG

Imagine climbing a mountain with two colleagues, Rose and Joel. Your goal is to plant a flag at the top of the mountain, and you are responsible for carrying most of the equipment to get you there. You start your climb, and about a quarter of the way up, you hear Joel cry out in pain. As a beginning climber, he made a mistake in his footing and accidentally twisted his ankle on a rock. "It's not serious," he says, "but you must go on without me."

Joel reaches into his bag and takes out his two-way radio. "I'll use this to keep in touch," he said. You and Rose say goodbye to Joel, and you keep climbing.

A couple of hundred feet later, Rose begins to huff and puff. She is clearly exhausted and slumps down on the ground. "I thought I could do this, but I guess I'm not ready," she says, looking longingly down the mountain. "I'll wait here, and you continue without me. I've got my two-way radio," she said. "I'll let Joel know I'm coming down."

You look up and believe the mountaintop is well within your reach. As you ascend, you find that the steepest grades are behind you now. Finally, you reach the top, joyfully. As you behold the wonderful view of the surrounding mountains, you feel pride and accomplishment. After all this time planning for this moment, you've made it. Time to plant the flag. Since the ground is so rocky, you reach into your backpack for a spade and find it's not there. You realize Joel has it, somewhere down the mountain. Oh well, you think to yourself, I can use something else to dig. But then a terrible feeling hits you...

Rose has the flag, and she's even further down the mountain by now. Why didn't she use the two-way radio to tell you she had the flag?

And then your heart sinks when you realize something even more distressing. Your two- way radio isn't in your backpack either. You have no way to keep in contact with Rose and Joel.

You shake your head and scold yourself. You have made the climb, outperformed your colleagues, but still can't complete the mission because they each have a piece of what you need to complete it. And you're mad at yourself too. If you had made sure you were in communication with them at all times, you would be victorious.

Arriving at retirement without a solid network is a little like the experience just described. You will have reached your destination, but may not be thoroughly equipped to move forward without the contributions of those who have gone before you.

When you arrive at retirement, wouldn't you like to be prepared?

Along the way to retirement, you have made wonderful contacts and met talented, resourceful people. They may have been entry-level, like Joel, or very experienced, but not quite at your skill level, like Rose. However, every one of them has something to offer you when you hit retirement age.

If you're reading this chapter, you probably have been in the workforce for some time. You may be in retirement itself, or quickly approaching it. Are you excited or fearful?

Some people dread retirement, afraid it will be a period of rapid decline into uselessness. They worry that the loss of daily work will lead to a dulling of their memory and other cognitive functions.

For others, it can be a period of new adventures, either of their own choosing or forced by their spouses or families. For example, I've received calls from spouses and grown children who speak of their recently retired matriarch or patriarch who is perfectly healthy but has too much free time on their hands and needs "to get out of the house." The NCG Factor is particularly helpful in these cases.

Then there are those for whom retirement is actually a transition into another career. After all, retirement doesn't always happen at age 65. For people in the military, education, government, sports, fashion, some of the arts and other professions, retirement happens at so early an age that beginning a new career is a necessity.

For example, when he retired at age thirty-four, former Chicago Bear's tight end Desmond Clark was the team's number two in all-time receiving yards, receptions and touchdowns. When I met him, I knew he could make a successful transition to a new career in financial planning. Dez remembers...

"Larry was one of the first professionals I connected with after retiring from the NFL. He taught me the art and value of networking. Sitting in on one of his LinkedIn seminars, then meeting with him one- on-one, opened my eyes and

heart to how I could create meaningful relationships with intentionality, authenticity, and a focus on helping other human beings prosper."

Desmond's transition to a new career went smoothly, but to make that transition during retirement, he needed the NCG Factor.

Regardless of where you fall in your attitudes about your impending or current retirement, no one can escape the inevitability of entering this new phase of life. The NCG Factor can help you increase your network, secure a legacy and be remembered by everyone you have known throughout your life. But first, you must have a network and preferably, a strong one. So, where do you fall on the spectrum? Do you have a solid, established network or could you use a few more contacts? And why is it so important to be concerned about NCG if you are no longer going to be engaged with the workforce? Let's find out.

YOUR NETWORK FOR RETIREMENT

One major difference between "networking" and applying the NCG Factor is that networking will help you in the business world while the NCG Factor will help you for life by building life-changing relationships. In retirement, you may or may not have a need for job referrals or professional mentoring. But if you have applied the NCG Factor, you may have the opportunity to help others who may call you to coordinate a project with a cause you care about or to ask if you know of a position for their friend in transition. You may be a mentor or coach to your children or grandchildren when they need a job or help them in some other way through your relationships.

I have had professionals attend my LinkedIn speaking events and have found that a number of them were retired. When I asked them why they were attending, even though they were retired, the most common response has been, "I want to help others and thought LinkedIn could help me to expand my network."

Think about it. You have spent a whole lifetime working towards the rewards of retirement. Maybe you have founded a company and recently transitioned out of it, or maybe you have been with the same organization for twenty-five years. In either case, you may have potentially met, befriended, and worked alongside hundreds of people. Think of how many of those people you could probably help at this point with your knowledge and expertise. Think of who your network may know that may be able to help you?

Now ponder what happened to those people and relationships. Are there any you can reach out to and ask for favors and advice? In other words, your inner circle? Or are people more distant from you now and it would feel awkward to contact them?

From the beginning of this book we have reiterated the idea that NCG is a way of looking at your human connections that is other-focused, instead of self-centered. Therefore, if you have networked, connected, and given to others to create life-changing relationships, you will enter retirement with lots of people in your network (if not only your inner circle) who will still be happy to make positive contributions to your personal life even though you have left the workforce.

Suppose you or your spouse is diagnosed with a rare medical condition which requires the attention of an elite specialist. You have one recommendation from your primary care physician, but you want to get a few opinions from the "best of the best." You research online but would feel more secure choosing a doctor if you had a recommendation. If you have a strong network, one way you could potentially find the perfect physician would be to reach out to your inner circle and see who they know or could recommend. A few years ago, I was referred by my physician to a specialist, the "best of the best." When I called for an appointment, I was told he wasn't taking any new patients. I reached out to a very powerful inner circle relationship in the healthcare industry and he knew the CEO of the hospital where this doctor spent most of his time. Within a few days, I received a call to meet with the physician the following week.

The request obviously has nothing to do with business, but if you have built a solid inner circle, nobody in it would find it odd that you reached out to them. Your inner circle would also willingly help you fulfill requests from others. For example, you may be searching for internship opportunities for a niece or nephew, to fill board positions for a friend's worthwhile charity, or to speak at a colleague's CEO event.

Sounds good, doesn't it? Even in retirement, you can continue to help people and they can continue to help you. However, your ability to interact productively with your network in near or full retirement has everything to do with the strength of your network. So, you must ask yourself and answer honestly...how strong is my network?

MY NETWORK IS STRONG!

If you have a strong network, it means that you not only have connections to people, but you also have well-defined inner and outer circles (Chapter 4) with many people who you can reach out to for help and who would do the same for you. Inside your network, you have a reputation for being a giver and it is how people will most likely remember you. Within your network, you also have a history of helping people and are beloved and admired for it. Does that sound like you? Then you may have been applying NCG all your life without consciously knowing it.

Congratulations! You are ahead of the game. You now have a wonderful place to start reaching out to others to help you achieve your retirement goals, whatever they may be. One of the major benefits of having a strong network as you head into retirement is to leverage your connections to help you achieve what you desire. Lucky for you, you've already done the hard part—building your network. Now you can start leveraging it.

MY NETWORK NEEDS WORK!

After a lifetime of working, many people find that they retire without a strong network. Why? In many cases it is because they have been in a position so long, they did not feel the "need to network." For others, it was simply not required for their job, so they never gave much thought to the matter. Both of these situations, while understandable, can easily be remedied with a little work on improving their NCG Factor.

If you are heading towards retirement and feel that your network is not strong, I invite you to take another look at Chapter 7 which discusses how to begin building and strengthening your network under **"I haven't had the time to build a network."** There you will find tips and hints on how to build your network. Doing so will make it easier to carry out most of the suggestions in this chapter.

NCG IN RETIREMENT

Whether you have built a solid network or are working on doing it now, retirement is a time of tremendous opportunity if you choose to embrace it, and the NCG Factor can help you however you decide to spend those years. People have as many retirement plans as there are retirees, but here are some of the most common retiree types and what the NCG Factor can do for each of them. Most likely, you will recognize yourself in more than one of the descriptions. However, in all of them, you can clearly see how leveraging your network with the NCG Factor can contribute to having the type of retirement you have always dreamed about.

The leisurely retiree. This retiree has been waiting all their life to retire! They have plans to spend more time with family, play more golf, and travel. They have little interest in continuing to stay engaged in the business world. Can you see how this type of retiree may benefit from the NCG Factor? They can reach out to their network to find...

- Recommendations for travel spots and/or referrals to people who can help them with travel arrangements, groups, etc.
- Other retirees with whom they have shared interests (for example, they can reach out to their network to find a retired golfer's group, or a prayer group at their church)
- Help for family members (For example, a grandchild may be exploring careers and need to talk to someone in her field of interest, a brother may need help selling a business, or a fellow retiree may be looking for a consulting job.)
- Bucket list experiences

The professional retiree. This individual may be retired, but their heart is still in the business world. They have no intention of spending their days on the golf course. They want to stay engaged with their industry. Most likely, they have a strong network. They may have started a business and executed a succession plan to enter retirement. Others are just so passionate about their industry and have done so much over the years to affect it that they do not want to abandon it. Still others have strong emotional ties with their professional network through trade associations or clients and want to continue building the relationship in some capacity. These individuals have amassed an amazing amount of knowledge over the years and want to share it with others. They also may be very entrepreneurial. So how can this retiree use the NCG Factor to meet their retirement goals? By leveraging their network, they can...

- Stay connected with former leaders and colleagues at their past employer
- Stay abreast of changes in their industry
- Share knowledge through emails and posts
- Discover consulting opportunities
- Offer to speak at events
- Find networking meetings, conferences, and seminars where they can stay engaged and continue to build their network
- Research places they could guest post an article on a topic they know well
- Find help with writing a book about their life as an industry expert
- Find mentorship opportunities
- Find open positions on executive boards that can use their expertise
- Find an enjoyable part-time position without regard to pay

The giving retiree. This retiree has one main objective in their retirement years: to give back. Throughout the years, they may have been approached with opportunities to help others but passed them up because they were "too busy" in their career. Now, with more time on their hands, they no longer have the pressures and time constraints that once kept them from helping out others and making a difference to their favorite causes. For the giving retiree with a strong network, they undoubtedly have plenty of people that they would be able to help, and can immediately delve into their network to find...

- Philanthropic opportunities
- Charities or organizations seeking board positions
- Speaking opportunities
- Mentorship opportunities
- Volunteer opportunities at their children's or grandchildren's schools
- Help launching programs, non-profits, or organizations to help others
- Connections to local, state, or national politics and causes of interest
- Opportunities to participate in organized events, programs, and rallies to strengthen awareness for a cause

The transitional retiree. This is the "young" retiree who, because of the constraints of their career, must now seek a different place in life. Perhaps their original career depended upon their youthful vigor in appearance (like modeling), stamina (like athletics), contractual obligation (the military) or lifestyle (global travel) and situations have changed. They most likely are changing their career and following a plan B that had been in the back of their mind since they started working. These retirees should refer to Chapter 7 and all the advice already offered to people in transition.

THE LEGACY

Regardless of what type of retiree you are, what goals you have in retirement, or how strong your network is, know that the NCG Factor creates legacies. If you are already known as a giver, your legacy will be solidified even further by doing even more good during retirement. If you are not known as a giver, but perhaps even a taker (see Chapter 3) there is still time to rewrite your legacy.

I have found that the NCG Factor is the most prolific tool I have to give to others and by using it regularly, you too can spend your retirement networking, connecting and giving to others to make the world a better place for everyone in your family and your network.

Have a pleasant, productive retirement!

THE NCG
ACTION LIST

Are you ready to put NCG into action in your life?

You took the first step and you read my book! Now it's time to see how the concepts I've presented can make a difference in your life and rewrite your legacy as a true giver to others.

1) **Reflection:** It's time to reflect on your life and determine what aspects of The NCG Factor are going to be most important to implement based upon the stage of your life or career (i.e. college freshman, new graduate, 20-year career veteran or 25 years and facing an elimination of your position). Look back at Chapters 6-8 to find inspiration for your particular time of life.

2) **Inner/Outer Circles:** Do you know who is in your Inner and Outer Circles? Start to define those relationships and continue to redefine and leverage them. Continue doing so as your network grows, throughout your lifetime, from college to retirement.

3) **Create your Introduction:** Follow the templates shared in the Appendix to create your own introduction. This will help you when you need to introduce yourself and will also help you to be a better connector and ask more easily for introductions. Share the template with your network too when they request introductions!

4) **Become a Connector:** Think about how you can make an impactful connection from one person to another while in college, at your current job, or even in retirement. Outside of work, help someone in transition to connect to a hiring manager. You can do it!

5) **Can you be a "Giver?":** Take a philanthropic path: It doesn't matter whether you are in college or deep into your career, if you have knowledge, share it. Become a mentor (formally or informally), volunteer for a charity or join a charity board. Do something for others!

6) **Do the Research/Build Your Social Presence:** Leverage LinkedIn, YouTube, Facebook, Instagram and Google. Take the time to research people you meet at your own company or in a 1:1 networking meeting, networking event, etc. Who are your common connections and interests? Take the time to do the research, because it could transform a networking connection into an inner circle addition.

7) **Set Goals:** What do you want to accomplish once a day or once a week? Remember, I said that my goal was to help someone in transition every week, even if it's over the phone or in person. If I miss a week, I help at least two people the next week. What is your goal?

8) **Network Strategically and with Purpose:** Learn how to meet new people early in life and don't stop! It's also never too late to start networking! You can ask your inner and outer circles for introductions to people they think you should meet. If you are connected to connectors, they will introduce you to new people and people you want to know. Have a goal and purpose for every 1:1 meeting or those you will meet at an event.

9) **Rewrite your legacy:** How do you want to be remembered? How would you be remembered today if this was your last day on Earth? You can rewrite your legacy by becoming an astute networker, connector, and giver. Read and re-read the chapters in this book. Adopt The NCG Factor in your life, and you can change not only your life but the lives of others and build real life-changing relationships.

10) **Pay-it-Forward:** Share The NCG Factor! This book is an opportunity to shine as a "Giver." If you are a teacher, purchase copies of this book for your students. Or purchase this book for your children, clients, friends. Help others in your inner and outer circles and those that will join those circles change their legacy in life!

Find the NCG Factor in your life and start building life-changing relationships today!

APPENDIX
HELPFUL NCG TOOLS

Now that you have learned the value of NCG itself and how to use it throughout your life to build life-long relationships from college to retirement, let's explore exactly how to do that.

When I realized the true power and value of connecting people to people, I decided it was important to take creative control of how people introduced me to other people and conversely, how I introduced people to others in my network. If we have a request, we must acknowledge that everyone is very busy, and we need to make it as easy as possible for them to help us. Also, when we are asked to make an introduction, for example, to help a friend connect to a hiring executive for a job they are interested in at a company, it's nice to have a system already in place so we can use our time as efficiently as we can on behalf of someone else.

As my friend Zori mentioned in Chapter 3:

"One tip Larry taught me that I found particularly helpful was to draft my own introduction to share with those I was asking to make introductions for me. This saved them time and shifted the work of explaining who I am and what I do to me."

Drafting your self-introduction is an important first step in creating a process to give and receive introductions. If you're not sure how to write an introduction that appears written by someone else, think about how you would like to hear others describe you. That would be the basis for the self-introduction you would provide for others to use.

Remember when you write your own introduction, make sure you include not only your work experience but any special connection you may share with the contact. These can include common interests or experiences, such as a hobby, a university, or interest in a charitable organization. This will "warm up" the introduction for you and make your first personal encounter with them more comfortable.

At the time I wrote this book, I was sending the following pre-written introduction to people who were willing to introduce me to others in their network. It was my basis for having others introduce me as well as introducing myself.

TEMPLATE A

My Self-introduction Template for someone else's use

I hope all is well. I would like to introduce a trusted peer of mine, Larry Kaufman. Larry has a stellar reputation in Chicago and in other markets across the country. (Insert your title, something brief about your company or what you do, something in common with the desired contact such as a school, hobby, sport or mutual acquaintances) He and his company are helping companies with their Accounting/Finance, Tax, Risk Advisory, Project Solutions & Consulting, Professional Resourcing, and Direct Hiring needs. Larry is also a global published keynote speaker on LinkedIn, an investor and advisor to a number of technology startups, and on the board of a respected charity, Holiday Heroes. (Share a philanthropic focus/ interest, etc.) He is a connector with an unbelievable network and a very giving person. Expect to hear from Larry to coordinate next steps. (End with a follow up or next step that you will take)

Once your introduction is set, you can now use it to send to people to help you meet others.

WHEN YOU ARE SEEKING AN INTRODUCTION

Let's say you looked at Tom's contacts and found someone you would like to know. Tom is in your inner circle and willing to make introductions for you, so you only need to contact him. Following is an email template that I use when I ask others to facilitate an introduction for me based upon someone they know directly. I may find out through this request that they are not as close to the connection of interest and then I would ask another connection in my inner/ outer circle that knows that person. I always ask the sender to cc: me in every email so the desired connection has my email to reach out to me. I also let the other person know they can use this version of my introduction or modify it as needed.

TEMPLATE B

Request an Introduction Email Template

Dear Tom,

I noticed you are connected to (insert name of desired contact). I would be very interested in an introduction. Could you make one for me? To make it as easy as possible, I have included something below that you can use to introduce me and you are welcome to modify it or use it as is.

(Insert your self-introduction from EXHIBIT A)

Also, please cc: me when emailing him/her. Thank you in advance for your help and let me know if I can help you in any way.

WHEN YOU WANT TO INTRODUCE YOURSELF

In general, it is always preferable to be introduced to a desirable contact by someone else. It's the wingman theory. If someone else can testify that you are worthwhile company and person to know, the new contact will be more receptive to meeting or speaking with you.

However, there will also be times where you meet someone who asks you to follow up with more information about you. While you can simply connect to them on LinkedIn, you might find a personal response more appropriate. Here is a useful template to use for those situations.

TEMPLATE C

The Self-introduction Template

Dear XXXXX,

I hope all is well. It was a pleasure to meet you/speak with you at the (insert place/time you met the person). As I mentioned when we met, (insert self-introduction in first person, like this:) I have a stellar reputation in Chicago and in other markets across the country. (Insert something in common with the desired contact such as a school, hobby, sport or mutual acquaintances) I help companies with their Accounting/Finance, Tax, Risk Advisory, Project Solutions & Consulting, Professional Resourcing, and Direct Hiring needs. I am also a global keynote speaker on LinkedIn, an investor, and advisor to a number of technology startups, and on the board of a respected charity, Holiday Heroes. (Share a philanthropic focus/interest, etc.) I strive to excel at networking, connecting, and giving.

I would welcome the chance to meet and discuss how we might help each other. Are you available next week for a coffee or phone call? I will contact you soon to confirm.

Whenever you are sending an invitation, or any correspondence for a request, always close with a firm intention to follow up with them in the near future.

WHEN SOMEONE ASKS YOU FOR AN INTRODUCTION

When I am asked to help facilitate a connection with someone in my network and I am able to make it happen due to my relationship with them, I always ask the requesting individual for their introduction. After all, they are about to receive a phenomenal and possibly life-changing introduction from me; they will certainly comply by helping this way. Also, by asking them to provide their own introduction, they have the opportunity to provide one that is more accurate and complete than any I could possibly ever write for them.

TEMPLATE D
Introduction Email Template

Dear XXXX,

Please allow me to introduce (name of person introducing).

(Insert the person's self-introduction. Offer to share EXHIBIT A with them if they need an example. Be sure it includes their name, title, other professional information about them, reason the introduction may be valuable and your expectations of meeting each other).

I have cc:'d (person's name) on this email so that you two can connect. He is someone you should meet. Expect to hear from (name of person) to coordinate next steps.

CALLING OR LEAVING A VOICEMAIL TO INTRODUCE SOMEONE

Sometimes it's just more efficient to call someone and ask them to make an introduction for you. In these cases, it's helpful to have a phone call or voicemail template readily available. Here is one I typically use if I decide to initiate an introduction first by telephone.

TEMPLATE E

Phone Call / Voicemail Template

Hi Tom,

I just noticed you are connected to (insert name of desirable contact). I would be very interested in an introduction from (yourself or someone else). Hopefully it's ok if I send you an easy-to-use, pre-written introduction to send directly to him. Thank you for your help and please let me know if I can help you in any way.

Any of these templates can be modified for your own personal use.

TEMPLATE F

The Transition E-Mail Template (Inner Circle)

Dear XXXXX,

I hope all is well. I appreciate our relationship (maybe share a customized reference of that relationship.). I really need your help. Due to (share the reason for your career transition, graduating from College, Chapter 11, Corporate HQ Relocation, etc.) I find myself in transition. I thought this email would help you to help me. However, I want you to know if I can ever help you or those you know, please never hesitate to ask. (it's important to share your interest in helping, which goes both ways).

I am searching for a (share the title and title variations of the roles you are searching for: CEO, President, CFO, Chemical Engineer, General Manager, etc.) in the following industries (share all applicable industries). I am open to relocation (or not open to relocation). The following companies are of interest to me as well (list out 5-10 companies). I am also interested in meeting people employed in similar roles and industries as they could be a great source of job leads for me. If you know someone hiring for positions aligned in companies/industries referenced, please feel free to call me directly to discuss or you can facilitate an introduction through email. I included my introduction below that you can use or modify to make the process easier for you. (include your email introduction template from Template A). I have also attached my resume (and/or handbill, generic cover letter, etc.). I will keep in touch on a regular basis during my transition, so you keep me top of mind. Thank you again for your friendship and support.

I would send every few weeks until you find your next job and always remember to thank your inner circle for their support.

TEMPLATE G

The Transition E-Mail Template (Outer Circle)

Dear XXXXX,

I hope all is well. I know it may have been some time since our last contact (maybe share a customized reference of that last contact or maybe it was fairly recent.). Due to (share the reason for your career transition, graduating from College, Chapter 11, Corporate HQ Relocation, etc.) I find myself in transition. I thought this email would help you to help me. However, I want you to know if I can ever help you or those you know, please never hesitate to ask. (It's important to share your interest in help, which goes both ways).

I am searching for a (share the title and title variations of the roles you are searching for: CEO, President, CFO, Chemical Engineer, General Manager, etc.) in the following industries (share all applicable industries). I am open to relocation (or not open to relocation). The following companies are of interest to me as well (list out 5-10 companies). I am also interested in meeting people employed in similar roles and industries as they could be a great source of job leads for me. If you know someone hiring for positions aligned in companies/industries referenced, please feel free to call me directly to discuss or you can facilitate an introduction through email. I included my introduction below that you can use or modify to make the process easier for you. (include your email introduction template from Template A). I have also attached my resume (and/or handbill, generic cover letter, etc.). I will keep in touch on a regular basis during my transition, so you keep me top of mind. If the frequency becomes an issue, please let me know (This is your outer circle, and they may not want regular communication or mind like your inner circle). Thank you again for your friendship and support.

I would send every few weeks until you find your next job and always remember to thank your inner circle for their support.

I hope these samples will inspire you to go forth and apply the NCG Factor to your life. It has made a tremendous difference in mine, and I know it will in yours also. From college to retirement, you can never go wrong building stronger, more productive relationships with those you meet yourself and through others, in-person or virtually. We have a lot to offer each other and NCG proves it!

Best wishes in all your NCG endeavors!

Larry Kaufman

ABOUT THE AUTHOR

 Larry Kaufman is a connector, giver, and rainmaker who lives his life to help others succeed. He is a Senior-Level Sales & Operations Leader and has been a globally-published speaker and trainer on LinkedIn for more than a decade. Larry has held roles in sales and operational leadership with P&L ownership, outside sales, and worked in other entrepreneurial capacities for the past several decades. He has hired and developed inside and outside sales forces in healthcare, technology, staffing, manufacturing, consulting firms, and the accounting industry. Larry has also been a powerful force in helping small, mid-market, and larger companies recruit talent to their organizations and has provided hundreds of corporate introductions to companies and business professionals wishing to expand their client base.

Larry is an investor and advisor to several local technology companies and sits on the board of Holiday Heroes, a charity that brings joy and a sense of normalcy to hospitalized children.

Larry resides in a Chicago suburb with his wife and two children.

Made in the USA
San Bernardino, CA
05 August 2019